To Know Him

A Christian Discipleship Book

Andrew Peters

TO KNOW HIM
First published 2003
2nd Edition 2013

© Andrew Peters 2013

Published by A.E. & L.A. Peters Outreach Enterprises
PO Box 225, Mansfield LPO. QLD Australia 4122
Website: www.outreachenterprises.com.au

Scripture quotations from the following version:

National Library of Australia Cataloguing-in-Publication entry
        Peters, Andrew, author.
        To Know Him: a Christian Discipleship book / Andrew Peters
        Edition: 2nd edition.
        ISBN: 9780975008195 (paperback)
        Subjects: Christian Life.
                Discipling (Christianity).
                Jesus Christ.
                God (Christianity)
        Dewey Number: 248.4

TABLE OF CONTENTS

Andrew and Lynette Peters

Andrew has had experience in the areas of youth ministry, evangelism, community care, pastoral ministry, leadership and teaching. He began his ministry as an evangelist, in the mid-seventies, as Director of Evangelism for Teen Challenge, in Kings Cross. He continues to preach on the cutting edge of youth ministry and evangelism today.

In the area of pastoral ministry, he has ministered in various leadership capacities in the Anglican Church, including being a member of Bishop-in-Council, and a Rector/Priest-in-charge (Senior Pastor) for over twenty years. He became Ministry Development Pastor of Garden City Christian Church, Brisbane at the turn of the millennium and has worked extensively in the area of the mobilization and development of lay ministry in the Church.

In recent years he has been engaged in the area of training and teaching. He has served as Lecturer and Head of the Faculty of Ministry Formation for Southern Cross Bible College (Richmond), as well as becoming Principal of Garden City College of Ministries and College of Arts, at the turn of the millennium. He has experience in the area of accreditation and management of both TAFE level and University level Ministry Training Colleges, as well as in the education and training of pastors, missionaries, performing artists and lay ministers.

Andrew currently shares his time between being Priest-in-Charge St Jude the Apostle Anglican Church at Everton Park, and consultancy work in the area of leadership development and strategy for organizations, colleges and churches. He completed doctoral studies with the ACU, with his Ph.D. dissertation on *The Effect of the Emerging Paradigm of Diversity on the Church and its Leadership.* The dissertation has been published as *The Emerging Paradigm of Diversity* and is available at: Amazon.com.

Lynette has had extensive experience in the area of music and worship, having over 20 years of experience as a music pastor, establishing and developing bands and worship teams in a number of churches. She plays the flute and keyboard and is a trained musician with 20 years teaching experience in both instrumental music and theory. Lynette works on the cutting edge of new paradigm ministry and draws forth the skills and abilities of worship leaders and musicians. Lynette was the Assistant Director of Garden City College of Arts and was instrumental in its establishment, accreditation of its courses and the development of its staff and students. Lynette is currently the Creative Arts Director at St Jude the Apostle Anglican Church, Everton Park, where she has been growing the various bands as well as developing the areas of drama, dance and music in the life of the church. Lynette has a Master of Music at Queensland University of Technology with her project in the area of performance anxiety.

INTRODUCTION

First Audience

This book was written for two different audiences. Initially it was written for those who are new to the Christian faith and experience. If that is you, then its purpose is to help disciple you as a new Christian and to help you understand the things of God and His kingdom. Your initial commitment to Jesus is the beginning of a journey that goes on for eternity. The early stage of this journey is an important time of learning so that you make it all the way. One of the greatest gifts Jesus has given to you is abundant life. Jesus said, *"The thief comes only to steal and kill and destroy; I came that they may have life, and have it abundantly."*[1] Abundant life is a quality of life we receive here, as we follow Jesus and grow in our relationship with Him. It is also a life that has no 'use by date.' It goes on forever. Jesus gives us this abundant life when we have invited Him into our life (and heart) as our Lord and Saviour. It is important to make the learning aspect of your Christian experience a high priority in your life, because the things that you will learn now will help you grow and be strong in your relationship with God. It will also make sure that you are not mislead by the manipulative workings of the devil and his friends, who like the thief mentioned above, only wishes to rob you of all the good things God wants you to enjoy. This book was written to help you understand God and His ways.

Second Audience

Concerning the second audience, this book was written for those who have become Christians sometime in the past, but have had no discipling or very little discipling in their lives

---

[1] John 10:10

11

since they made that initial commitment to follow Jesus. If that is you then there will be some things about God and His Kingdom that you do not know. Also there will be some things that you do know that have not made enough sense for you to actually go and do them. Because you have not known how to do some very fundamental and basic things in your relationship with God, the fruit of that relationship has been very meager indeed. You will have had great difficulty in maturing in God and becoming strong in faith. The devil will have twisted things in your life to such an extent that you do not know whether you are coming or going. You will feel that the devil is constantly on your back instead of at your feet. The sense of having abundant life will either be a fleeting thing that visits every now and then, or mundane in its outworking in your life. To change your situation you are going to have to learn again some very basic and fundamental truths about God, His Kingdom and you. This book was written to help you understand God and His ways.

God Bless You
Ps Andrew Peters

CHAPTER ONE

THE ONE AND ONLY TRUE LIVING GOD

Our picture of God affects the way we live our lives and the way we treat other people. A true understanding of the nature of God produces in us a true understanding of ourselves, our worth and our abilities. There is more to us than simply being "material people living in a material world." It also enables us to see others, as people to be loved and cherished, rather than things to be used and abused. Respect and self-worth does not arise from a belief that we are just flesh and bones, as some atheistic evolutionists would suggest. If we are simply flesh and bones, then there is no valid reason why we should respect and care for others, let alone there being any reason why we should think of ourselves as important and worthwhile.

If we could adequately explain who God really is then God is probably not worth knowing. However, just because we cannot contain God entirely in our thinking doesn't mean God doesn't exist or that we cannot know Him. Throughout history we have seen individuals, groups, nations and entire cultures believe in and fight for their understanding of God. For some, God meant a variety of gods contending with one another for our attention, with perhaps one of them seen to be the chief god. Many of the nations that surrounded the nation of Israel, in the early part of her history, fell into this category. The gods would take male and female forms, with goddesses being prolific in many cultures. This was also common amongst the super-power nations of those times leading up to and including the Roman Empire that was in control of Palestine during the days of Jesus. Some nations included human leaders amongst the gods, as did the Greek empire since the time of Alexander the Great; the Roman Empire with its Caesars; and the Egyptians with their Pharaohs. Apart from the nation of Israel, very few, if any other cultures or nations believed in only one God. Yet it is that one God who has proven to be true in every sense, both in philosophical and theological terms, to be the God who created and established the universe and the world upon which we dwell.[2] In our day there is once again a plurality of gods clamoring for our attention. Many of these come to us through New Age propaganda or through Eastern Mysticism. Apart from these there are now three distinct religions that believe in only one God: Judaism (Israel), Islam (Moslem) and Christianity. However, the nature of that one God is quite different in each. Unique also to our modern culture is an extensive belief in atheism. Something that was rarer in previous stages of history.

EVOLUTIONARY ATHEISM:

There are those who would argue that we are simply the result of an evolutionary process that has occurred over hundreds of thousands of years. Not only that but the evolution of human

---

[2] In the past the term universe meant "all existing things; all creation; world or earth; cosmos; all mankind." (The Australian Pocket Oxford Dictionary, 1976). Throughout this book the term will be used with that extensive meaning: referring to all that exists in the created order. It does not include the infinite nature of God, who is over and above the created order. However, there is some discussion in scientific theoretical circles as to whether or not our universe is one of many universes. Andrew Chaikin notes, "There's a reason some theorists *want* other universes to exist: They believe it's the only way to explain why our own universe, whose physical laws are just right to allow life, happens to exist. According to the so-called anthropic principle, there are perhaps an infinite number of universes, each with its own set of physical laws. And one of them happens to be ours. That's much easier to believe, say the anthropic advocates, than a single universe 'fine-tuned' for our existence." (Editor, Space & Science posted: 07:00 am ET 05 February 2002)

beings, along with all other animals, birds, and sea creatures occurred through a process that was separate from and devoid of any influence or activity of an entity called "God." Much scientific evidence is claimed for these arguments. However, despite the seemingly acceptance of the Theory of Evolution to be evolutionary fact, there is still little evidence to substantiate the theory to be true. In science a theory is a suggestion or proposition that has not yet been proven by the evidence available.

When sufficient evidence is collated to prove the theory to be true then it becomes a "law" (e.g. the Law of Thermodynamics) or "principle." When Darwin proposed the Evolutionary Theory in the 1850's it was as a suggestion to explain certain physical evidence that he had collated. In over 150 years of scientific research, with massive attempts to prove the theory to be true, no evidence has yet been found that conclusively proves the theory to be right. It still remains a theory, not a law or principle. There is no evidence that proves the transition between one type of species and another, which lies at the crux of the evolutionary theory.

Irrespective of the lack of such evidence, the Atheistic Evolutionary Theory itself does not explain why certain fundamental things operate in this world. It does not, and cannot explain the intricacy of the human body and the way it operates, nor can it do so for the plant world or the animal kingdom. The claim that this world and all it contains is simply an accident in time, with no other force at work except chance and impersonal matter, does not explain anything. Even if there was sufficient evidence to suggest that the Evolutionary Theory was true, it still does not deny the existence of God. It simply means that God created the world in process. The philosophical framework that has built itself around the Theory of Evolution leaves us with certain disconcerting conclusions:

- **Impersonal World:** the word is impersonal – for we simply arrived as an accident in time related to a combination of chance, time and impersonal matter.

- **Material People:** we are material people living in a material world - Madonna's "Material girl."

- **No Spiritual Realm:** the material is all that exists – there is no spiritual realm.

- **Death is an end:** so let's eat, drink and be merry for tomorrow we die.

- **Human person has no value:** there is no valid reason for human beings to think they are important or have value – we are simply an accident in time. Others are to be used for our own pleasure and advancement. This life is all that there is - so get what you can while you can.

PANTHEISTIC GOD – EASTERN MYSTICISM

Pantheism is the foundation of most Eastern religions, such as Hinduism and Buddhism, with the Hari Krishna movement being an offshoot of Hinduism. The Pantheistic view of God sees the origins of the world in terms of a God who formed all things out of itself. This Pantheistic God cannot be noted as being personal but is rather an undefinable, impersonal, philosophical absolute.[3] In Pantheism not only is God every-thing, but everything in the universe and beyond is a part of this God. God is the universe and the universe is God. Thus all things, both good and evil are part of God.

To speak of good and evil, right and wrong, justice and honesty, and the like is quite redundant, for the use of these terms are quite meaningless because everything is God. The

---

[3] B. Wilson, *The Best of Josh McDowell, A Ready Defense*, (Thomas Nelson, Publishers, Nashville, 1993) p.274

difficulty in interpreting Eastern Mysticism is the many forms and developments that both Hinduism and Buddhism have taken. Whereas some have tried to personalize an underlying impersonal nature of God, it has usually occurred by the elevation of a person to the divine, rather than an original concept of a living personal God, who made both the heavens and the earth. Pantheism again leaves us with certain disconcerting conclusions:

- **God is impersonal:** Hinduism's Supreme Being is the indefinable, impersonal Brahman, a philosophical absolute. In Transcendental Meditation (TM) it is noted that "Everything in creation is the manifestation of the unmanifested absolute impersonal being, the omnipresent God."[4]

- **We are all part of the universal God:** Hinduism views human beings as a manifestation of the impersonal Brahman, without individual self or worth. In Transcendental Meditation (TM) it is noted that "Each individual is, in his true nature, the impersonal God."[5]

- **Death is a recurring event:** reincarnation is an endless attempt to make yourself good through an ongoing process of death and rebirth, with the new state of the rebirth related to your conduct in the previous life.[6] There are no real guarantees and the pain of repeatable deaths holds no real hope.

---

[4] B. Wilson, *The Best of Josh McDowell, A Ready Defense*, (Thomas Nelson, Publishers, Nashville, 1993) 274, 276.

[5] *The Best of Josh McDowell, A Ready Defense*, 276, 355.

[6] *The Best of Josh McDowell, A Ready Defense 352-353* "Salvation in Hare Krishna is thoroughly entwined with the Hindu concept of karma, or retributive justice. This teaching, which requires belief in reincarnation and/or transmigration of the soul, says that one's deeds, good and bad, are measured and judged either for or against him. Only when his good deeds have "atoned" for his bad deeds (and he is thus cleansed of this evil world) can he realize his oneness with Krishna and cease his cycles of rebirth."

- **Human person has little value:** human Beings have no real value or true rights in this religion. Since both good and bad are part and parcel of the Pantheistic God, there is no distinction between right and wrong. It is not that there is no recognition of good and bad, but there is no way to determine whether one or the other is right or wrong. This leaves human beings with no grounds upon which to think they are important and of value. It thus leaves them open to abuse and without justice.

CREATOR GOD

The Biblical God is a Creator God and existed before everything else in the Universe, both in the seen world (the material world) and the unseen world (the spiritual world). The Creator God created everything that exists, *ex nilo,* out of nothing and everything that this God created was created intrinsically (basically) good.[7] God is independent of this creation and stands over and above His Creation. This is called God's "transcendence." At the same time this Creator God has an ongoing relationship with the world that He made and the human beings He created in His own image and likeness. God is also intimately involved in His Creation (this is called God's "immanence"), but He is not the creation and the creation is not God. This view allows human beings to see in the world and Universe the nature, goodness, and beauty of God Himself

---

[7] Andrew Chaikin, Science Tuesday, (Ed), Space & Science posted: 07:00 am ET 05 February 2002, note from the realm of scientific theory, "To understand why, you have to go back to the Big Bang, that mysterious, mother-of-all-explosions that most astronomers believe spawned our universe. One second, according to theory, there was nothingness. The next, our cosmos sprang into existence. Nature seems to have pulled off the feat of getting something -- in fact, everything -- for nothing." Craikin refers to nature as the originating power behind all that exists, but only a Personal, Infinite, Living God, separate from but intimate with His creation can explain all that we find in nature.

and allows men and women to find true and valid worth. The Christian Creator God leaves us with certain encouraging conclusions:

- **God is Personal:** this Creator God is intensely personal and communicates, interacts and develops relationship with human beings, who are also intensely personal. He is separate in being from the created order, but interacts with that creation on a personal level. God is good and contains no evil in Himself.

- **People are both Material and Soul/Spiritual**: human beings are spiritual, soulical and material beings, and they operate on all three of those levels.

- **Spiritual realm**: there exists both a material realm and a spiritual realm. God dwells in the spiritual realm and interacts in the material realm. Human beings can communicate with both the material and spiritual realms.

- **Death is not the end:** There is life after death that exists eternally and human beings, having left their mortal bodies in this world take on immortal bodies in the next.

- **Human Beings have value:** human beings are of great importance and value because they are created in the image and likeness of God. Evil is not something that is intrinsic to the creation but occurs as a result of actions taken by created beings, both angels and humans. There is a distinction between good and evil; right and wrong. The individual person is as important as the whole human race.

THE NATURE OF GOD

How do we know which God is which? Who is the God who is there? From our understanding of the world we live in and our own human nature and character, the God who is really there must contain three aspects within Himself that are reflected in the Creation He made. These are unity, diversity and personality.

Unity: There is throughout the world an incredible unity that indicates a common source. There is an oneness or sameness within the nature of this world. This can be seen in the consistency of maleness and femaleness throughout the majority of living species.

Diversity: At the same time there is also an extensive diversity or individualism within the world we live. This can be seen in the case of falling snow, where no two snowflakes are exactly alike in their make-up. We also see it in the uniqueness of fingerprints or DNA, where no human being has the same fingerprints or DNA as anyone else.

Personality: men and women are personal beings and have personal relationships. We thus can speak in terms of love, affection, honor, respect, success, failure and the like. There is an intense level of personality in the created order.

These three characteristics are not only fundamental aspects of the world we live in, but are also fundamental to our own beings and lives. So fundamental that they cannot be forgotten in any discussion about the nature of God and His encounter with the men and women He has created. Thus we would expect to see within the nature and being of this God these three characteristics. Although each of these religions propose certain of these aspects, only one believes in "One God" who has all three of these characteristics as part and parcel of the nature and being of God – *Christianity.*

Judaism: lies at the beginnings of the Christian Faith, but falls short of a full and complete revelation of the nature and being of this God, because of their rejection of Jesus Christ. It is not so much that they rejected Jesus Christ as their Messiah, the one promised and sent by God. It was because God's chosen Messiah was in fact His one and only Son. What the Jewish leadership rejected was the revelation of God Himself in the Son of God. Judaism certainly holds a strong belief in the unity of God that is His oneness. It also holds a strong picture of the revelation of God as a personal God who interacts and communicates with human beings. What it lacks is the sense of diversity within God Himself, a diversity that is strongly reflected in the creation He made, and the Messiah He sent.[8]

Islam: is a revision of aspects of Judaism and Christianity with new insights proclaimed by the Prophet Muhammad, born in Mecca in Arabia in A.D. 570. The followers of Islam are known as Moslems. Islam claims that there is only one true God whose name is Allah. Allah is portrayed as all-knowing, all-powerful, and the sovereign judge. Yet Allah is not a personal God, for he is so far above man in every way that he is not personally knowable.[9] Islam acknowledges the unity of the God who is there, and though Allah has on occasions interacted with human beings on a certain level, Allah does not build relationships with them. It also denies any diversity in the nature and being of the God called Allah.

Christianity: Christianity arose out of Judaism through the revelation of the Jewish Messiah in the person of Jesus Christ. Jesus not only fulfilled all the expectations of the Jewish Messiah, but also went way beyond them in that He was not simply a man chosen and sent by God. He was Himself God who took human form. It is the Christian belief in a Trinitarian God

---

[8] It is not that the Jewish monotheistic understanding of God is devoid of diversity, as it conceives of both the word and spirit being divine aspects of God's nature, but that it does not explicitly address this concept. Andrew Peters, *The Emerging Paradigm of Diversity: Its Effect on the Church and Its Leadership* (Mansfield, QLD: A.E. & L.A. Peters Outreach Enterprises, 2013).

[9] *The Best of Josh McDowell, A Ready Defense,* 308

that reflects the unity and diversity that we find in the world, as well as the personality we find in human beings. The Christian belief in God as Trinity states that there is "one God" and thus establishes the unity within that God. But it also states that within that one God there are "Three Persons", the Father, the Son and the Holy Spirit, which establishes the diversity within that One God. It is also the Christian God who continually reveals Himself as a personal God, who relates to men and women on a personal level and desires them to relate to Him. He is also described as having the characteristics we attribute to personality and personal relationships. He thus loves, grieves, cherishes and gets angry. Only the nature of a Personal God can explain this particular uniqueness we find in the nature of men and women.

GOD AS TRINITY

God is One: Christians are "monotheists." Like Jews and Moslems they believe in only "One God."

God as Three Persons: Where Christians dramatically differ with Jews and Moslems is that within that understanding of the nature of the "One God" there are three persons, the Father, the Son and the Holy Spirit. Each of these Persons is Divine and can rightly be referred to as God. Although we usually call Jesus the Son of God, we must always remember that Jesus Himself is also God. His Sonship refers to His relationship to God the Father, not to us. Each of the Persons of the Trinity is a distinct person, and yet at the same time is inseparably (undividedly) linked to the others. When one of them acts, all three of them are acting together.

God as Father: First, God is the "Father." God the Father gives us an understanding of the almighty nature of the God in whom we believe. It was God who created the world we live in and the Universe that surrounds it. The use of the word "Father" for God comes from God Himself. It is God's way of showing us in the first instance, the relationship He has with His Son Jesus, and in the second, the type of relationship He wants to have with us.[10]

God as Son of God: Jesus is the "Son of God" who took human form when he was conceived and born of the Virgin Mary, His Mother. Jesus came into the world, from heaven that we might see and understand the true nature of God and His love for us. Jesus was both "God" and "Man," and through Him we see the invisible nature of God. Whereas, the Father is seen as the Creator of the world in which we live and all that surrounds it, Jesus is seen as the one through whom the world was created. He is also seen as the "Redeemer" of mankind, in that He came into the world and died on a cross to save us from the eternal effects of our sin and rebellion. The word "Redeem" means to buy back for a price. He bought us back from the dominion of Satan and the shackles of sin in order that we might live in freedom and have eternal life. Jesus' death and resurrection from the dead shattered these chains of oppression in our lives, as well as defeating the threat of death.

God as Holy Spirit: The Holy Spirit is the third Person of the Trinity who comes to make God real to us. It is the Holy Spirit who works in our lives to transform us to be like Jesus. He works to help us live our lives for God and to follow in God's ways. It is the Holy Spirit who brings the love of God into our hearts that we might truly love others. The Holy Spirit is a distinct Person of the Godhead and not simply God's power or force. However, when He comes into our lives He brings to us the power we need to serve God in this world and to testify to the true nature of God and proclaim salvation in Jesus Christ.

---

[10] The use of the name father for God comes primarily from Jesus. Whereas the Old Testament uses the name father for God about five times, usually in reference to God as the father of the fatherless, Jesus uses the name father for God about 100 times in John's gospel.

DISCUSSION QUESTIONS: GOD

1. How does our picture of God affect our use of people and love of things?

2. If God was impersonal, how would that affect our value of ourselves and others?

3. What other signs of unity and diversity do we find in God's creation?

4. Do you know people who you would consider "impersonal"? How would our lives be affected if we were all impersonal?

5. Why do you think it is important for God to be both personal and to interact intimately with human beings?

6. If God is "spirit", how does that affect our understanding of the relationship between the physical or material realm and the spiritual realms?

7. How does our understanding of God change and impact our perception of death?

CHAPTER TWO

THE WORD OF GOD

God is a God who speaks and when He speaks things happen. He speaks in a number of ways and in a variety of circumstances and situations. He spoke at the beginning of time. As a result the extensive and immense Universe came into being out of nothing. He spoke again and the world upon which we live came into being. Then God created the trees and plant life, fish and sea life, animals and bird life, and finally human beings. All these things were created through the words He spoke (Genesis 1). The God who speaks is the God who made us and the God who sustains our life in this world.

He is a God who interacts with men, women and children and desires to have a living relationship with them. The Bible is a record of this interaction between God and human beings. The Bible portrays a picture of a God who pursues a relationship with His people, even when they desert Him, ignore Him and disobey His commands. The Bible too is called the "Word of God." Its words and pages are inspired by His influence and record the relationship He developed with Israel, who came to be His People. A relationship He intends to develop with us in an even greater way, for the promises He gives to us are far greater than any that were promised to them. The Old Testament contains these stories.

The New Testament notes another way in which God's Word comes to us and speaks into our lives. It records the story of God speaking into our lives through Jesus Christ. Jesus is also called the Word of God, and is a far greater presence of His Word than has ever come to human beings before. For in the person of Jesus Christ the living Son of God came into this world in human form. We call this coming the incarnation of the Son of God.[11] Jesus was not only the Word of God but as the Word of God He reflects the very being of God Himself. Jesus reveals the incredible love that God has for us and His desire for us to have a living and vibrant relationship with Him (see Hebrews 1).

A Christian is a person who has a living and dynamic relationship with God the Father, through Jesus Christ the Son, in the power of the Holy Spirit. We come to the one and only living God, who is one God in three persons: the Father, Son and Holy Spirit. It is that God who you have responded to by asking Jesus Christ to come into your life to be your Lord and Savior. It is that God who knows your heart and your ways and loves you anyway. It is that God who has spoken down through the ages, over thousands of years, to people just like you. It was that God who spoke to you, when you heard Jesus Christ call you to follow Him, and invited you to become a member of His family. On His behalf we welcome you to the Family.

God's speaks to us by a myriad of means so that we can understand His purpose for our lives. He speaks the Word of God to us through a direct audible voice, through the quiet still voice of the Holy Spirit within us, through preachers, teachers, angels, study groups, other Christian people, and through reading the BIBLE. The following are some of the ways its words touch our lives:

The Word of God Will Stand Forever

Both the Old and New Testaments tells us that though the heavens and the earth might be destroyed and disappear, the word of God will always be there. There have been periods of history when the people carried out an intense campaign to destroy all copies of the Bible. Not only did their efforts fail, but

---

[11] Incarnation refers to the divine son of God become a human person in Jesus Christ.

they themselves have long passed away, whilst God's Word continues to speak into people's lives across the world today.

The grass withers, the flower fades; but the Word of our God will stand for ever (Isaiah 40:8).

Jesus said, 'Heaven and earth will pass away, but my words will not pass away' (Matthew 24:35; Mark 13:31; Luke 21:33).

The Word of God is Truth

There are two things that Jesus referred to as the *truth*: one was Himself and the other was the Word of God. Truth here does not just refer to telling the truth, and not lying, but also refers to the very foundation or basis of reality and life. It is what gives substance to our lives and confidence that not only is there a God, but the God who is really there is reliable and true.

Jesus said, "I am the way, the truth and the life; no one comes to the Father but by me' (John 14:6).

Speaking to God the Father Jesus said, 'Sanctify them in your truth, thy word is truth' (John 17:17).

When Paul writes to Timothy he refers to the Word of God as *'the word of truth'* (2 Timothy 2:15) and to Titus he calls it the *'sure word'* (Titus 1:9). Proverbs tells us that the Word of God always proves true,

Every word of God proves true; he is a shield to those who take refuge in him. Do not add to his words, lest he rebuke you, and you be found a liar (Proverbs 30:5-6).

The Word of God is the Sustenance (Food) of Life

The word of God is as important for our health and wellbeing as the food we eat. We cannot prosper as a Christian without God's Word.

Jesus said, 'Man does not live by bread alone, but by every word that proceeds from the mouth of God' (Matthew 4:4).

The Word of God and Eternal Life

Both Jesus and St Peter tell us that the words of Jesus are the words of eternal life. The Word of God plays an important role in our salvation and coming into the experience of new life in Jesus, which goes on for eternity. For it is through our believing in our hearts that God raised Jesus from the dead, and the confession of our mouths that He is our Lord, we are saved.

Peter says to Jesus, 'Lord, to whom shall we go? You have the words of eternal life' (John 6:68).

Jesus said, 'It is the spirit that gives you life, the flesh is no avail; the words that I have spoken to you are spirit and life' (John 6:63.).

But what does it say? The word is near you, on your lips and in your heart (that is, the word of faith which we preach), because, if you confess with your lips that Jesus is Lord and believe in your heart that God raised him from the dead, you will be saved. For man believes with his heart and so is justified, and he confesses with his lips and so is saved (Romans 10:8-10).

The Word of God and Creation

The Word of God had an active part in bringing into existence both the heavens and the earth, for through the Word of God all things were created.

In the beginning was the Word, and the Word was with God, and the Word was God. He was in the beginning with God; all things were made through him, and without him was not anything made that was made. In him was life, and the life was the light of men. The light shines in the darkness, and the darkness has not overcome it (John 1:1-5).

By the word of the LORD the heavens were made, and their entire host by the breath of his mouth (Psalm 33:6).

They deliberately ignore this fact, that by the word of God heavens existed long ago, and an earth formed out of water and by means of water (2 Pet 3:5).

The Word of God and Our Lives as Christians

It is through the Word of God that we are made pure and clean before God, and the Word of God plays an important part in our walk with God. Through the Word of God and our meditation upon it, along with our obedience to its commands we are able to continue in holiness and purity,

Jesus said, 'You are already made clean by the word which I have spoken to you' (John 15:3).

How can a young man keep his way pure? By guarding it according to thy word... I have laid up thy word in my heart that might not sin against thee (Psalm 119:9-15).

The Word of God Abides in You

For us to truly live as Christians then the Word of God must become a part of our lives, part of our very nature and personality. We are called to have God's Word abiding and dwelling in us. It has to be engrafted into our very nature and personality and become a spontaneous response in our lives and actions,

Therefore put away all filthiness and rank growth of wickedness and receive with meekness (humility) the implanted word, which is able to save your souls (James 1:21).

Let the word of Christ dwell in you richly, as you teach and admonish one another in all wisdom (Colossians 3:16).

Jesus said, 'If you continue in my word, you are truly my disciples, and you will know the truth and the truth will set you free' (John 8:31-32).

Obey and Hold Fast to the Word of God

We are called to hold fast (that is, to cling to it with all our strength and might) to the Word of God and to obey its commands. Without obedience to God, everything else we do as Christians is of no value. Above everything else God wants our obedience.

Everyone then who hears these words of mine and does them will be like a wise man who built his house upon the rock; and the rain fell, and the floods came, and the winds blew and beat upon that house, but it did not fall, because it had been founded on the rock. And every one who hears these words of mine and does not do them will be like a foolish man who built his house upon the sand; and the rain fell, and the floods came, and the winds blew and beat against that house, and it fell; and great was the fall of it (Matthew 7:24-27).

But be doers of the word and not hearers only, deceiving yourselves (James 1:22-25).

Holding fast the word of life, so that in the day of Christ I may be proud that I did not run in vain or labor in vain (Philippians 2:16).

But whoever keeps his word, in him truly love for God is perfected. By this we may be sure that we are in him (1 John 2:5).

All Scripture is Profitable

The words of the scriptures (the Bible) speak to us about every area of our lives.We are called to heed the words of the scriptures: to read, digest and obey its words in order that we might be equipped for every good work.

All scripture is inspired by God and profitable for teaching, for reproof, for correction, and for training in righteousness, that the man of God may be complete, equipped for every good work (2 Timothy 3:16-17.).

You will prosper in all you do

God delights to see His servants prosper in all areas of their lives and ministry (Psalm 35:27). God desires to bless and prosper you in all that you do. Such prosperity comes to those who do two things: first, they guard their hearts from those who would speak negative things into their lives and lead them away from the things of God. Second, they meditate, digest and learn the Word of God and put it into action. The man or woman who does those two things will be fruitful in all things in their right season. That means that it doesn't simply happen overnight. We must persist in such activities and we will reap a harvest of prosperity.

Blessed is the man who walks not in the counsel of the wicked, nor stands in the way of sinners, nor sits in the seat of scoffers; but his delight is in the law of the LORD, and on his law he meditates day and night. He is like a tree planted by streams of water, that yields its fruit in its season, and its leaf does not wither. In all that he does, he prospers (Psalm 1:1-3).

You Shall Bind These Words to Yourself

We are called to have the Word of God in our hearts and souls, to keep them and to teach them to our children.

You shall therefore lay these words of mine in your heart and in your soul; and you shall bind them as a sign upon your hand... and you shall teach them to your children, talking of them when you are sitting in your house, and when you are walking by the way, and when you lie down, and when you rise (Deuteronomy 11:18-19).

The Word of God Helps Us Mature

The Word of God plays an important part in our growth as Christians. It is as that word becomes a part of our hearts that we become strong in God; can defeat the dirty tricks of the evil one, Satan; overcome the circumstances that face us; and bring the reality of heaven into the struggles we go through on earth.

I am writing to you, little children, because your sins are forgiven for his sake. I am writing to you, fathers, because you know him who is from the beginning. I am writing to you, young men, because you have overcome the evil one. I write to you, children, because you know the Father. I write to you, fathers, because you know him who is from the beginning. I write to you, young men, because you are strong, and the word of God abides in you, and you have overcome the evil one (1 John 2:12-14).

For though by this time you ought to be teachers, you need someone to teach you again the first principles of God's word. You need milk, not solid food; for everyone who lives on milk is unskilled in the word of righteousness, for he is a child. But solid food is for the mature, for those who have their faculties trained by practice to distinguish good from evil (Hebrews 5:12-14).

DISCUSSION QUESTIONS: THE WORD OF GOD

1. What are some of the ways the Word of God can come to us?

2. How long will the Word of God stand?

3. What two things did Jesus refer to as the truth? What is truth?

4. Apart from bread what does man need to live?

5. Whose words are the words of eternal life?

6. By what are all things created?

7. What helps us to continue in holiness and purity?

8. What must the Word of God become in our lives?

9. Who are we to obey?

10. What is profitable?

11. In what part of us does the Word of God dwell?

12. In Psalm 1 what does the man do with the Law of the Lord?

13. Write out verse 14 of Psalm 19.

14. Write out Hebrews 4:12.

15. Write out Romans 10:8.

Chapter Three
Sin and Rebellion & Salvation

The Dignity of the Person

The scriptures give us a picture of the human person that indicates an oscillation between intense dignity and deep depravity. The Genesis story describes men and women as the pinnacle of God's creation, made in the image and likeness of God and as such were created "very good" (Genesis 1:26f). As such they have the capacity to operate on three levels of consciousness covering the spiritual, soulical and physical dimensions of existence (Genesis 2:7). Men and women are described as intelligent beings, having the power of rational thought, a capacity to reason things out and come to logical conclusions, in both their relationship with God and with other human beings (Isaiah 1:18).

Men and women are seen as moral beings, having the capacity to recognize the difference between right and wrong. They are able to make free moral choices and in relationship to God they have the freedom to say yes to God as well as no (Deuteronomy 30:19). More than anything else men and women are described as spiritual beings that have the capacity to know and enjoy fellowship with God (Genesis 3; John 4:24). The Genesis story notes the state of grace, innocence and peace the man and woman had with God and with one another (Genesis 2:25; 3:8). There at the beginning there existed an intimate relationship between God and them, and between one another. However, these relationships were not to last as sin entered into the world and the lives of men and women.

The Fall of Mankind – A Journey into Depravity

Sin came about through one man's disobedience to the Living God. Sin then impacted every living creature that has inhabited this planet and its environment. The Genesis story goes on to describe this disobedience and its results: the fall of men and women[12] from that state of grace and peace with God, and from their original state of dignity and innocence, into a state of depravity (a state of corruption and wickedness)[13] and despair. Adam and Eve represented the human race in both their relationship with God, as well as at "the temptation" that came by the Devil (referred to as the serpent in the story). The temptation was not simply an instigation to disobey God's commands, but also to exalt themselves above God.

Having sinned against God, by disobeying His word, they fell into a state of rebellion and arrogance (pride), which resulted in a deep enmity between them and God. The word "state" indicates a change to a way of "being" that has deeply impacted our personality and souls and brought immense damage to our spirits. This shift in "state of being" brought about a loss of innocence and peace for both the man and the woman, and produced a deep sense of guilt and shame (Genesis 2:25). The Genesis story goes on to describe an ever-outworking process of depravity beginning with the slaying of Abel, by his brother Cain, to the time of Noah when God regretted ever having created men and women, due to the depths of their depravity (Genesis 4:8; 6:5,6; Psalm 14:1-4). This change in spiritual

---

[12] 'Men and women' here is used in a generic sense to represent mankind as an entity, not simply Adam and Eve. For what the first man and woman did in the Genesis story was then passed down to all who followed them.

[13] The word depravity is used in this chapter to refer to wickedness and moral corruptness (The Australian Pocket Oxford Dictionary 1976). Though men and women moved into a state of depravity, this is not meant to infer or imply that men and women are to be considered to be totally depraved in all that they do. Though it is possible for men and women to become totally depraved, as the Noah motif seems to indicate (Genesis 6:5-8), there is still within the human person the glimpse of the likeness and image of God. After all God found in Noah someone who was worthy (Genesis 6:9).

condition - from innocence and peace to rebellion and
arrogance - impacted all men and women in subsequent
generations of every nation and ethnic group (Romans 3:23;
5:12, 19; Isaiah 53:6; 1 John 1:8-10).

LOSS OF RELATIONSHIP

One of the greatest impacts of this shift in state of being, from
righteousness to sin, was the destructive influence it brought
to their relationship with God and with one another. This shift
in spiritual condition severely damaged the relationship men
and women had to God. The eventual effect was to separate
men and women from the presence of God and place them
outside the benefits of His Kingdom (Isaiah 59:1-2; Genesis
3:10; Isaiah 59:1-2; Romans 8:7-8)). They were subsequently
described as spiritually lost and dead. They became spiritually
dead through their trespasses and sins, and subsequently lost
from the Kingdom of God (Ephesians 2:1; Genesis 2:17; 3:24;
Romans 6:23; 8:6; Ephesians 2:1; James 1:15). This shift in
spiritual condition also impacted the inner person and brought
into their lives the bondage to sin, which is expressed as a deep
bondage to self or selfishness (James 1:14; Galatians 5:19-24).
Finally, it impacted the relationship men and women have
between themselves, along with disharmony with others
(Genesis 4:8; Colossians 3:5-9).

SIN AND REBELLION

The word 'sin' basically means to "miss the mark." In archery
missing the mark means the arrow failed to hit the bulls-eye.
Sin means to have "fallen short of" or "failed to achieve" the
goals and standards that God has laid down for us. These goals
and standards are laid down in the Bible, and upon our
"consciences" which are an essential part of our beings and
nature. Sin is essentially a "principle" at work in our lives that
leads us away from the goals and standards God has set down

for our lives. Though this principle of sin is not a part of our basic nature, it is so ingrained upon our personalities and natures that its power and influence over the things we do and think are enormous. In fact, it is a dictator that rules our lives, overthrowing the influence of our God and consciences upon our actions and decisions.

This principle of sin is at war with God, fighting against what He is trying to achieve in our lives and resisting God's purpose for us. Sin leads us into conflict with God and cuts us off from His presence and love. Not only does it set us at odds against God but it also tries to prevent God from trying to heal the breach (separation) that has occurred between Him and us. Sin also urges us to resist God's influence in our lives and calls us to flee from His love and care. Sin paints a false picture of God that shows Him as a boring Dictator in the sky who only wants to spoil all our fun and enjoyment. The problem with sin is we believe what it tells us and we flee from the loving care and presence of God our Father.

SIN PRODUCES DEATH

Sin produces death in this world and eventually eternal death in the world to come. It is an enemy we must face and deal with because it robs us at every level of our life. In the Genesis story we find two particular trees identified by God as crucial to the life and future of the human race. The first tree was the "tree of life." God intended human beings to enjoy eternal life with Him. The tree of life was their means to live eternally with God, within the new world and universe that God had created. It was a tree of abundance and life that both Adam and Eve were encouraged to eat, as it would provide an eternal sustenance for them.

However, the Genesis story tells us of another tree, resident in the garden – this one called the "tree of the knowledge of good and evil." God told the man he was not to eat of the tree of the knowledge of good and evil, "for in the day that you eat from it you will surely die" (Genesis 2:17). It was the fruit of that tree that was used by the Devil to tempt Eve to disobey God and eat. However, the essence of the temptation was to doubt not only God's word but also His goodness. The Devil told Eve that God was keeping something from her that would give her real understanding. He intimated that it would make her like God Himself. Eve bought the deal and taking the fruit of the tree she ate it and then encouraged her husband to eat too (Genesis 3:1-6).

In the eating of the fruit their eyes were opened, but they did not become like God. Their whole perspective on life and how they saw themselves changed significantly and the intimate relationship they had with God and with one another was shattered. Prior to the temptation we are told that they lived naked and were not ashamed. After the temptation and their disobedience to God's command, we are told,

Sin's Impact produces:

❖ **Estrangement from God** (Genesis 3:10; Isaiah 59:1-2; Romans 8:7-8)

❖ **Bondage to self - selfishness** (James 1:14; Galatians 5:19-24)

❖ **Disharmony with other people** (Genesis 4:8; Colossians 3:5-9)

❖ **Spiritual death** (Genesis 2:17; 3:24; Romans 6:23; 8:6; Ephesians 2:1; James 1:15)

"and they knew they were naked; and they sewed fig leaves together and made themselves loin coverings. When they heard the sound of the Lord God walking in the garden in the cool of the day, the man and his wife hid themselves from the presence of the Lord God" (Genesis 3:7-8).

41

They now saw themselves as sex objects, not persons, so nudity became a matter of embarrassment and fear. The ties of love and loyalty snapped as the man tried to justify his failure by blaming his wife. The woman's experience of childbirth was now spoiled, for now she would bear her children in pain (Genesis 3:12-13, 16).[14] As well as this she saw the deep and intimate relationship she had with her husband turn from companionship to potential serfdom (Genesis 3:16). Sin brought death to their spiritual relationship with God and its intimacy; it brought death to their personal self-worth; and it brought death to the intimacy of their own relationship. Sin continued to impact men and women bringing death to relationships, communities and nations. Sin eventually brought physical death, as well as a loss of eternity.

RESULTS OF REBELLION

After their rebellion, and fall from grace and innocence, the Genesis story tells us that the man and the woman were excluded from partaking of "the tree of life." 'Then the Lord God said, "Behold, the man has become like one of Us, knowing good and evil; and now, he might stretch out his hand, and take also from the tree of life, and eat, and live forever... So He drove the man out; and at the east of the garden of Eden He stationed the cherubim and the flaming sword which turned every direction to guard the way to the tree of life"' (Genesis 3:22-24). The tree of life disappears from the Bible stories and the history of the human race until it is mentioned again in the book of Revelation, where it is found in the new heaven and earth, and located in the New Jerusalem. "through the middle of the street of the city; also, on either side of the river, the tree of life with its twelve kinds of fruit, yielding its fruit each

---

[14]Ferguson, Sinclair B. and David F. Wright, *New Dictionary of Theology*, (Downers Grove, IL: Intervarsity Press) 2000, c1988.

month; and the leaves of the tree were for the healing of the nations" (Revelation 22:2).

The total effect of sin was to cut us completely off from God and separate us eternally from His love and compassion, His mercy and forgiveness. Sin's effect lasts for eternity, leading us into an eternal death from which there is no escape or salvation, except through Jesus Christ. Sin robs us of everything that God wants us to have and enjoy. However, God did not leave "Sin" in control. God made a way for us to be released from the shackles of sin and turn to eternal life through His Son. St Paul writes, "The wages of sin is death, but the free gift of God is eternal life in Christ Jesus our Lord" (Romans 6:23).

TEMPTATION TO SIN

It is important to note that temptation is not the same as sin. We are all subject to temptation to sin. Even Jesus Himself was tempted to sin by the Devil and yet He never committed any sin at all, either in thought or action. Temptation to sin nearly always comes to our minds first, although sometimes it can start by affecting our emotions. Thoughts of temptation to sin are not sin until we accept the temptation and act on it either in our thoughts and imagination or our actions. Our defense against temptation is to know God's word and use it against the tempter, the Devil. Look up Jesus' temptation in the wilderness to see how he dealt with temptation to sin and rebellion (Matthew 4:1-11; Mark 1:12-13; Luke 4:13).

OTHER WORDS FOR SIN

There are a number of different words used in the Bible for sin. Some have a slightly different meaning but all in some way or other refer to the work and influence of sin in our lives. These words are "iniquity", "transgression", "trespass", "debt", and "to go astray". Some of them refer to our disobedience to God's Law and Word, such as iniquity and transgression, while others refer to our going away from God and the things of His Kingdom either ignorantly or accidentally. However, all actions of sin are accountable to God. When we sin we throw ourselves into direct opposition to God and His purposes for our lives and for the world in which we live. The principle of sin working in our lives finds its expression in the things we think and then in the things we do. We will be found accountable for the things we have done, either of sin that leads to death, or righteousness that leads to eternal life through Jesus Christ.

REBELLION

Rebellion can certainly be included as sin against God. However, it has some qualities of its own that we need to study further. Rebellion is not only an action it is an attitude. A rebel is one who has rejected all authority except himself or herself. Rebellion is by far one of the most destructive types and expressions of sin because it rejects God's authority and position completely in our lives. It tells God that He has no right whatsoever in our lives and belittles what God thinks and commands. God compares rebellion to witchcraft and says that it is an abomination to him. God is quite compassionate with the sinner, one who fails to achieve the call and standard God has set. When it comes to the rebel, on the other hand, God resists the rebel and brings him or her down. Continually throughout the Old Testament we find God charging His people as rebels, a stiff necked people who were not willing to do as He asked and desired (1 Samuel 15:22-23).

STUBBORNNESS

Stubbornness is really only different from rebellion in degree. The stubborn person still recognizes to some degree God's authority in his life, but he only does what God asks and desires grudgingly, with his heels dug firmly in the ground. God has to coax or cajole (persuade) him or her into doing anything at all. He still obeys God but with moaning and groaning about how hard God is on him. God compares stubbornness to the sin of idolatry and once again says that it is an abomination to Him. God desires us to be willing people, willing to love, serve and honor Him (1 Samuel 15:22-23; Deuteronomy 18:1-10).

SALVATION THROUGH JESUS CHRIST

Despite sin's active influence in our lives God has done something to release us from its oppressive control. Through Jesus Christ God has set us completely free from the dominion and control of sin in our lives and from its eternal effect. Jesus came to take away our sins and to release us from the oppressive control and dominion of sin in our lives. Through His death on the cross and resurrection from the dead, Jesus Christ broke the chains and shackles of sin in our lives, releasing us so that we can live in righteousness towards God and achieve His goals and purposes for our lives (1 John 3:4-5; Matthew 1:21). Through Jesus Christ God has provided for us complete forgiveness for our sins, cleansing from our guilt and release from the eternal punishment for sin (Ephesians 4:32). Sin had left us destitute and without God in the world, separated and lost from His kingdom. God found us through Jesus and brought us home (Jeremiah 50:6; Ezekiel 34:4, 16; Luke 19:10; Matthew 10:6; 15:24; Luke 15).

NEW BIRTH

Jesus taught that because of the effect of sin and rebellion in our lives we all need to have a 'new birth' to enter into the Kingdom of God. We need to be "born again" or "born anew". This means that we have to have a new spiritual birth to enter the Kingdom of God and to become Christians. Jesus said, "Unless one is born of water and the Spirit, he cannot enter the Kingdom of God" (John 3:1-6). Just as we are born into this world, we also need to be born again into the Kingdom of God.

45

FORGIVENESS

One of the unique aspects of the Christian Faith is the "forgiveness of sins". The Christian God is a God full of mercy and compassion. He has compassion upon the people He has created and offers them freely the forgiveness of their sins, no matter how bad those sins have been. When God forgives our sins it means that He wipes the slate clean. He no longer calls to mind the things we have done that have been wrong. John writes "If we confess our sins, he (God) is faithful and just, and will forgive our sins and cleanse us from all unrighteousness" (1 John 1:9). Not only does God forgive us for our sins and wrong actions, He also takes away the guilt that plagues us because of the things we have done. He makes us clean and fresh inside, healing the effects our sins have had upon us.

Jesus placed one very important condition upon our receiving forgiveness from God. He said, "For if you forgive men their trespasses, your heavenly Father also will forgive you but if you do not forgive men their trespasses, neither will your Father forgive your trespasses" (Matthew 6:14-15). Jesus calls us to extend the same type of forgiveness to others as we have received from God. If we do not forgive them we will in turn lose our own forgiveness (Read the story of the unforgiving servant in Matthew 18:23-25).

NEW LIFE

Jesus said that He had come to give us life and that life abundantly (John 10:10). The life that He promised was God's life, the life that comes to us because we are part of His Kingdom, one of His Children. The life that Jesus came to bring us has two aspects. It is a quality of life that is God's life that sustains us, encourages us and empowers us for our life and work in this world. Secondly, it is a life that goes on forever; it is eternal life in the Kingdom of God. We are promised eternal life in God's Kingdom if we will believe in God's Son, our Lord Jesus Christ and if we will remain faithful to Him and His will for our lives. Jesus said, *"God so loved the world that he gave his only Son, that whoever believes in him should not perish but have eternal life" (John 3:16).*

Jesus also told us that the only way we can experience God's life is through and only through Jesus Himself. He said, *"I am the way, the truth, and the life; no one comes to the Father, but by me" (John 14:6).* Jesus also described himself as the "Resurrection and the Life". Jesus Himself is the source of God's life for us (John 11:25). Jesus is the only way to eternal life, the life that He gives to us here in this world and which goes on forever and ever. Paul writes, "For the wages of sin is death, but the free gift of God is eternal life in Christ Jesus our Lord" (Romans 6:23). The life of God that comes into our lives through Jesus is a life that brings a change and transformation to our lives. Paul writes,

> *Therefore, if anyone is in Christ, he is a new creation; the old has passed away, behold the new has come (2 Corinthians 5:17).*

When Jesus Christ comes into our lives he makes us new persons. He changes us and transforms us into the person He always intended us to be. He gives us His life, His love, His forgiveness, His peace, His joy and His affection, and He then sends us out to love and care for others in the same way He has cared for us.

DISCUSSION QUESTIONS: SIN AND REBELLION

List any words you do not understand.

1. What does the word sin mean?

2. What does sin mean in regards to the goals and standards that God has laid down for us?

3. Sin is essentially a .... working in our lives?

4. What does sin do to our consciences?

5. What does the principle of sin do concerning God?

6. What is the eternal effect of sin in our lives?

7. What has Jesus Christ done for us concerning sin?

8. Is temptation and sin the same thing?

9. Why is rebellion one of the most destructive types of sin?

10. In what manner does the stubborn person accomplish what God wants?

11. What does God think of rebellion and stubbornness?

12. What does God do to the proud person?

DISCUSSION QUESTIONS: NEW BIRTH, FORGIVENESS AND NEW LIFE

1. With what two terms does the Bible describe the non-Christian?

2. What did Jesus Christ come to do?

3. What did Jesus say we needed to have to enter the Kingdom of God?

4. What does it mean to have God forgive our sins?

5. What does God do with our guilt?

6. What condition did Jesus place on our forgiveness?

7. What are the two aspects of life that Jesus came to bring us?

8. Who is the only way to God the Father?

9. Who is the source of God's life for us?

10. When Jesus Christ comes into our lives what does He make us?

11. What does Jesus send us out to do?

CHAPTER FOUR

REPENTANCE, CONFESSION AND RESTITUTION

When we sin either in thought, attitude or action we separate ourselves from God and the life of His Kingdom. God has provided for us through Jesus Christ, complete forgiveness for our sins, cleansing from our guilt, and the healing of the breach (breakdown) that has occurred between Him and us. For us to enjoy the life of God's Kingdom there are three things that we need to do concerning our sinful thoughts, attitudes and actions. They are repentance, confession and restitution.

REPENTANCE

There can be no real release from the dominion of sin and the healing of its effect in our lives without repentance. God's love and kindness towards us is intended to lead us to repentance. God desires that all people, every man, woman and child, should come to repentance (Romans 2:4; 2 Peter 3:9). Jesus said, "the time is fulfilled, and the kingdom of God is at hand; repent and believe in the gospel (good news)" (Mark 1:15). We are all called to repentance.

THE MEANING OF REPENTANCE

Repentance is a change of mind, heart and purpose. It always involves a change for the better: a change from bad to good, from hatred to love, and from being self-centered to being God-centered. It is not merely to repent of and forsake sin, but to change one's mind, heart and attitude towards sin completely. Repentance involves seeing sin and rebellion for what it really is, to see it how God sees it, and wanting no longer to have anything to do with it because of its wrongness and destructive nature. Repentance involves seeing sin, rebellion and stubbornness as God sees it and having a Godly grief over sin and its destructive nature. Repentance is only real when it is done for the right reasons and motives. Godly sorrow and grief over sin produces real repentance, whereas worldly sorrow and grief produces death.

WORLDLY SORROW:

The motive behind worldly sorrow and grief is still self-centered and manipulative. We grieve and sorrow over our sins not because we are admitting the wrongness of our actions nor even being truly sorry for what we have done. We grieve because our actions and sins have hurt us. The things we have done have recoiled back upon ourselves in the form of rejection and punishment and we repent so that we might once again gain acceptance and approval from God and others.

GODLY SORROW:

Godly sorrow for sin sees our sins and actions for what they really are and the destruction they have wrought. We admit our sins and seek forgiveness because we see how wrong we have been and how much we have hurt God and other people. Repentance always involves a turning: a turning away from a selfish self-centered way of life, and a turning towards God to lead a Godly and God-centered way of life.

CONFESSION

We have a tendency to whitewash our sins. We tend to play down the wrongness of our actions and the destructive effect of those actions in our own lives and in the lives of other people. There can be no release from the guilt of our sins and wrong actions without confession. As long as we run away from taking full responsibility for the things we have done, we will never be free from the dominion of sin and its oppressive rule in our lives. We are responsible for what we do! No amount of provocation or temptation from others can justify the things that we do which are wrong. Just because others treat us badly does not excuse our actions and reactions. If we want peace with God and forgiveness for our sins then we need to stop blaming others for the things we have done.

Confession involves taking full responsibility for our actions and reactions. It involves facing up to our sins and wrong actions, thoughts and attitudes. It means admitting to God that we have been wrong and the things we have done are wrong and that we have hurt God and other people. In confession we admit to God the things that we have done that were wrong and we ask Him to forgive us for all that we have done that has hurt Him and other people. God promises that if we confess our sins to Him, then He is faithful and just and will forgive our sins and cleanse us from all unrighteousness. When God cleanses us He takes away the guilt we have felt over the things that we have done which have been wrong (1 John 1:9).

RESTITUTION

Often the reason people do not find release from their guilt and shame is because what they have done has not only offended God but has also offended and hurt other people. God not only expects us to confess our sins to Him and to make amends with Him, but also to go to those whom we have hurt and to make amends with them. As well as asking God's forgiveness we also need to ask the forgiveness of those whom we have offended. Jesus said, "So if you are offering your gift at the altar, and there remember that your brother has something against you, leave your gift there before the altar and go; first be reconciled (made friends again) to your brother, and then come and offer your gift" (Matthew 5:23-24). For instance we see in Luke's gospel Jesus challenge a man named Zacchaeus, who in response was moved to make restitution for all that He had done when He came to know how much God loved him, despite all that he had done. A natural outworking of his repentance was restitution.

> *And there was a man named Zacchaeus; he was a chief tax collector, and rich. And he sought to see who Jesus was, but could not, on account of the crowd, because he was small of stature. So he ran on ahead and climbed up into a sycamore tree to see him, for he was to pass that way. And when Jesus came to the place, he looked up and said to him, 'Zacchaeus, make haste and come down; for I must stay at your house today." So he made haste and came down, and received him joyfully. And when they saw it they all murmured, "He has gone in to be the guest of a man who is a sinner." And Zacchaeus stood and said to the Lord, "Behold, Lord, the half of my goods I give to the poor; and if I have defrauded any one of anything, I restore it fourfold." And Jesus said to him, "Today salvation has come to this house, since he also is a son of Abraham. For the Son of man came to seek and to save the lost' (Luke 19:2-10).*

Restitution means "to restore" or "to make right again". For instance if we have stolen something from someone and we were to make restitution: it would mean that we would return what we had stolen. In Leviticus 6:1-5 it is made clear that if we have stolen something from another person then we should return what we have stolen and also give them an extra 20% (1/5) of its value because of what we have done to them. For instance if we stole $100, we should return $120.

There are many things that we do which hurt other people and ruin our friendship with them. We cannot just brush it under the carpet and forget about it and hope that they will forget about it too. We need to make right the things we have done wrong. Often we need to ask that person's forgiveness for the way we have treated them. If we do not make things right again, not only will our relationship with them be strained and tense, but we will have no peace in our relationship with God. God will not allow us to just ignore the hurts and wrongs we have done to others and He will continue to niggle us about it until we make amends, until we make restitution. One caution though: when sin has simply been a matter of our thought life, especially sexual thoughts, we should not make restitution with, nor seek forgiveness from, others, unless they have been aware of the impurity of those thoughts.

CONCLUSION

If we will seriously deal with our sins and wrong deeds, repenting of them; making confession to God; and making restitution to others then we will be free from guilt and will feel the loving forgiveness of God our Father and the beautiful life of His Kingdom. We will have peace with God through our Lord Jesus Christ (Romans 5:1).

DISCUSSION QUESTIONS: REPENTANCE, CONFESSION AND RESTITUTION

1. What has God provided for us through Jesus Christ?

2. Who does God desire to come to repentance?

3. Repentance is a change of what?

4. What is repentance a turning away from, what is it that we turn towards?

5. What do we have a tendency to do with our sins?

6. Who is responsible for what we do?

7. What does God promise if we confess our sins to Him?

8. What does restitution mean?

9. What must we do about the wrong things we have done to others?

CHAPTER FIVE
BAPTISM IN THE HOLY SPIRIT

Throughout our lives as Christians we will experience the presence of God in many different ways. There are two particular experiences that we have as Christians that are directly related to the working of the Holy Spirit in our lives. The first of these experiences is what Jesus called being "born again" or "born anew". This experience of new birth is in fact the beginning of our Christian life when we are born again into the Kingdom of God. This new birth is a spiritual birth into the Kingdom of God that is brought about by the working of the Holy Spirit. This new birth is linked with our baptism in water and through it we are made members of God's Family and Church. Jesus said, "Truly, truly, I say to you, unless one is born anew, he cannot see the kingdom of God"; and again he said, "...unless one is born of water and the Spirit, he cannot enter the kingdom of God" (John 3:3,5). When we are born again into the Kingdom of God not only do we become Christians, but also the Holy Spirit comes and lives inside of us, in our hearts. From within us He works in our lives to help us to live as Christian People.

The second experience we have with the Holy Spirit is called the "Baptism in the Holy Spirit." It is also referred to as being "filled with the Spirit" and the "release of the Spirit". All these terms give us some indication as to the meaning of the baptism in the Holy Spirit. The word baptism itself means to be "totally immersed" or "saturated". It was originally used to refer to the dying of material a different color and to the sinking of a ship in the sea. When the word baptism is used to refer to the Baptism in the Holy Spirit it refers to an experience we have where God totally immerses us or saturates us in the Holy

Spirit. It is also called being "filled with the Spirit" because when we are baptized in the Holy Spirit our whole being is filled with the presence and power of the Holy Spirit. It is also referred to as the "release of the Spirit" because the Holy Spirit flows from within us to flood our whole being, body, soul and spirit. Jesus said, "He who believes in me, as the scripture has said, 'Out of his heart shall flow rivers of living water". Now this he said about the Spirit, which those who believed in him were to receive" (John 7:38-39).

When we are "born again" into the Kingdom of God, the Holy Spirit comes and lives in our hearts (our inner most self). When we are "baptized in the Holy Spirit the Holy Spirit floods our whole being with His presence and power. The Baptism in the Holy Spirit brings to us a greater awareness of the presence and working of the Holy Spirit in our lives. We become more sensitive to his presence within us and His guidance in our lives.

JESUS – THE ONE WHO BAPTIZES IN THE HOLY SPIRIT

The New Testament indicates that Baptism in Water is not the same as Baptism in the Holy Spirit, even though they may occur at the same time. When we are baptized in water it is God's Ministers who baptize us in the name of the Father, the Son and the Holy Spirit. When we are baptized in the Holy Spirit it is Jesus Himself who baptizes us. John the Baptist tells us that Jesus is the one who will baptize us in the Holy Spirit. He says, "After me comes He who is mightier than I, the thong of whose sandals I am unworthy to stoop down and untie. I have baptized you with water, but He will baptize you with the Holy Spirit" (Mark 1:7-8)

WHEN ARE WE BAPTIZED IN THE HOLY SPIRIT

In the New Testament we find Jesus baptizing people in the Holy Spirit in a number of different ways.

1. **Ephesus:** on one occasion, Paul baptized in water twelve disciples of John the Baptist at Ephesus. Paul baptized them in water and when they came up out of the water he laid his hands upon them and they were all baptized in the Holy Spirit (Read Acts 19:1-7).

2. **Cornelius's House:** on another occasion, Cornelius and his whole family and friends were baptized in the Holy Spirit while they were listening to Peter's sermon about Jesus. Later Peter and his friends baptized them all in water (Read Acts 10:1-48).

3. **Samaria:** on yet another occasion, the people of Samaria were converted through the ministry of Philip and he also baptized them in water. They later received the Baptism in the Holy Spirit when the apostles Peter and John came down from Jerusalem and laid hands upon them. When Peter and John laid hands upon them they were all baptized in the Holy Spirit (Read Acts 8:4-17).

The New Testament indicates that different people receive the Baptism in the Holy Spirit at different times in their lives. There are no hard and fast rules as to when we receive the Baptism in the Holy Spirit. What is certain is the Baptism in the Holy Spirit is an experience of the Holy Spirit that is promised to every person, whoever they may be. Peter when he speaks directly about the Baptism in the Holy Spirit says that it is the gift that God has promised to His People through the prophet Joel when Joel said, "And in the last days it shall be, God declares, that I will pour out my spirit upon all flesh" (Acts 2:16-17; Joel 2:28-32).

Peter then tells the people, when they asked him what they needed to do to be saved: "Repent, and be baptized every one of you in the name of Jesus Christ for the forgiveness of your sins; and you shall receive the gift of the Holy Spirit. For the promise is to you and to your children and to all that are far off, every one whom the Lord our God calls to him" (Acts 2:38-39). The promise of the gift of the Holy Spirit is given to every man, woman and child in the whole world and in every age. The early church recognized when people had been baptized in the Holy Spirit, by the gift of tongues that accompanied it. They saw it as an authentic part of the Christian life and experience.

SPEAKING IN TONGUES

On a number of occasions in the New Testament when people received the Baptism in the Holy Spirit they also received what was called "speaking in tongues". This speaking in tongues was a new prayer language that God gave to His People through the Holy Spirit. Through the use of this new language they were able to pray and worship God with their whole being (1 Corinthians 14:13, 15). On the day of Pentecost, when over a hundred of the disciples of Jesus, including the twelve apostles, were baptized in the Holy Spirit "they were all filled with the Spirit and began to speak in other tongues, as the spirit gave them utterance" (Acts 2:1-4). We also find that when Cornelius and his family and friends received the Baptism in the Holy Spirit that Peter and his friends, "heard them speaking in tongues and extolling God" (Acts 10:46). We also find Paul telling us that he continually prayed and spoke in tongues (1 Corinthians 14:18).

Paul tells us that when a person speaks in tongues he is praying with his spirit in a special language that God has given to him or her. Paul distinguishes between our praying with our minds and our praying with our spirits. When we pray with our minds we pray with our normal language, i.e. English for us, Greek or Hebrew for Paul. When we pray with our spirits then we use the special prayer language that God has given to us which is called speaking in tongues   (1 Corinthians 14:2, 14-15).

BAPTISM IN POWER

Before He ascended up into heaven Jesus commanded His disciples to remain in Jerusalem until they had received the promise of the Father, which was that they would be baptized in the Holy Spirit (Acts 1:4-5). On the Day of Pentecost we find them waiting in Jerusalem and they received the Baptism in the Holy Spirit (Acts 2:1-4). Jesus also told them that, "... you shall receive power when the Holy Spirit has come upon you; and you shall be my witnesses in Jerusalem and in Judea and Samaria and to the end of the earth" (Acts 1:8). From that small group of people who waited for the coming of the Holy Spirit and who received power when the Holy Spirit came upon them, the Church that we know throughout the world had its beginning. The same power that was given to them when they received the Baptism in the Holy Spirit is also given to us when we receive the Baptism in the Holy Spirit that we too can bear witness to our Lord Jesus Christ and what he has done for us and for the whole world. Jesus baptizes us in the Holy Spirit so that we can be effective in ministry, using the gifts given to us by the Holy Spirit for that ministry.

Discussion Questions: The Baptism in the Holy Spirit

1. What is the first experience we have with the Holy Spirit?

2. Where does the Holy Spirit come and live?

3. What is the second experience we have with the Holy Sprit?

4. The second experience of the Holy Spirit is referred to by what names?

5. What does the term "baptism" mean?

6. What does God do to us when He baptizes us in the Holy Spirit?

7. When we are baptized in the Holy Spirit what does the Holy Spirit flood us with?

8. Who baptizes us in the Holy Spirit?

9. Name three (3) times when different people are baptized in the Holy Spirit?

10. To whom does the New & Old Testaments say the Baptism in the Holy Spirit is promised to?

11. To whom does Peter say the gift of the Holy Spirit is promised to?

12. What is "speaking in tongues"?

13. What did the people use "speaking in tongues" for?

14. Paul tell us a person speaking in tongues was praying with what?

15. What did Jesus say the disciples would receive when the Holy Spirit comes upon them?

CHAPTER SIX
CHRISTIAN PRAYER

Prayer is communication! It is communication with God. It is a two-way relationship between God and us. It involves our speaking to God and our listening to what God wants to say to us. Prayer comes in many forms and types.

PRAYER AND THANKSGIVING

All prayer should begin with thanksgiving. Thanksgiving involves giving thanks to God for all He has done for us and for others. Thanksgiving is the gateway into the presence of God. There are times when we do not feel like thanking God and feel that there is nothing to thank Him for anyway. It is at those times that we need to give thanks to God more than ever.

Make a joyful noise to the LORD, all the lands! Serve the LORD with gladness! Come into his presence with singing! Know that the LORD is God! It is he that made us, and we are his; we are his people, and the sheep of his pasture. Enter his gates with thanksgiving, and his courts with praise! Give thanks to him, bless his name! For the LORD is good; his steadfast love endures forever, and his faithfulness to all generations (Psalm 100).

PRAYER OF PRAISE

There are five sacrifices that we can offer to God of which the sacrifices of praise and thanksgiving are the only ones that originate entirely from ourselves. Praise is different from thanksgiving because it involves telling God what we think about Him and how much we appreciate Him; not for what He has done for us but for who He really is to us. One of the easiest ways of praising God is through singing hymns and songs about God and to God. Our praising God through singing does not have to be only in Church, but can be anywhere we like. God likes praise and dwells in and inhabits the praises of His People. Praise with thanksgiving brings us into the very presence of God Himself. We are called to praise God in songs, psalms and melodies from our hearts.

> *Let the word of Christ dwell in you richly, teach and admonish one another in all wisdom, and sing psalms and hymns and spiritual songs with thankfulness in your hearts to God. And whatever you do, in word or deed, do everything in the name of the Lord Jesus, giving thanks to God the Father through him (Colossian 3:16-18).*

> *Rejoice always, pray constantly, give thanks in all circumstances; for this is the will of God in Christ Jesus for you (1 Thessalonians 5:16-18).*

PRAYER OF CONFESSION

Sin and rebellion separates us from God, it cuts off our lines of communications with Him. We are called to take responsibility for the things we do, both good and bad. When we do something wrong then we must admit it to God and ask Him to forgive us for the things we have done which are wrong and have hurt Him and other people. This is what confession of our sins is all about. When we have confessed our sins to God then we must stop doing the things that are wrong and turn to follow and obey God and to do the things He wants us to do. If we confess and admit our wrong actions (sins) to God, then He will forgive us for what we have done, cleanse us from all the wrong, and take away our guilt. John writes in his first letter:

> *If we say we have no sin, we deceive ourselves, and the truth is not in us. If we confess our sins, he is faithful and just, and*

will forgive our sins and cleanse us from all unrighteousness (1 John 1:8-9).

PRAYER OF FORGIVENESS

The Lord's Prayer is the most well-known and used prayer by Christians. It was that prayer that Jesus taught His disciples when they asked Him to teach them how to pray. Each time we pray that prayer we ask GOD to forgive us our sins AS we forgive those who have sinned or trespassed against us. When Jesus taught His disciples this prayer, He told them that unless they forgive those who have sinned or trespassed against them then their Heavenly Father would not forgive them. He said,

For if you forgive men their trespasses, your heavenly Father also will forgive you; but if you do not forgive men their trespasses, neither will your Father forgive your trespasses (Matthew 6:14-15).

If we do not forgive others then our Christian lives will be completely messed up. We will not be able to walk with God, to know His Presence in our lives, to understand His will for us, nor to know what it is like to be loved by God and to love Him with our whole mind, heart, soul and strength. If we hold bitterness, resentment, hatred and grudges (malice) towards any other person, then it will mess up everything to do with our relationship with God. We are called to forgive others as He has forgiven us.

And do not grieve the Holy Spirit of God, in whom you were sealed for the day of redemption. Let all bitterness and wrath and anger and clamor and slander be put away from you, with all malice, and be kind to one another, tenderhearted, forgiving one another, as God in Christ forgave you (Ephesians 4:30-32).

(Look up: Matthew 5:7; 6:12, 14-15; 18:23-35; Mark 11:25; Ephesians 4:32; Colossians 3:13).

PRAYER OF DEDICATION

We are called primarily to make God the first priority of our lives. We are to seek Him with all our hearts, to love, serve and obey Him all the days of our lives. Our relationship with God grows and strengthens as we continue to dedicate and offer our lives to Him. We need to continually make Him first in our lives and to confess Him as our LORD. There may often be times in our lives when our relationship with God grows cold and distant. At these times we need once again to give our lives to God and make Him the first and foremost Person in our lives.

If you confess with your lips that Jesus is Lord and believe in your heart that God raised him from the dead, you will be saved. For man believes with his heart and so is justified, and he confesses with his lips and so is saved (Romans 10:9-10).

(Look up: 2 Chronicles 7:14; Jeremiah 29:11-13; Matthew 6:33).

PRAYER OF INTERCESSION

The word "intercession" means to plead or speak on behalf of someone else. The "Prayers of Intercession" are those prayers that we pray to God for other people and their needs. We should pray daily for our family and friends; for our Church and its people; for our nation of Australia and our leaders; and for the world and the people of all nations. Two other words that are used for this type of prayer are "supplications" and "petitions". The meaning of these two words is similar. They mean, "to make request" on behalf of others and ourselves. Throughout the New Testament we are told to make prayers of intercession, supplication and petition, on behalf of others and ourselves.

For Others: *First of all, then, I urge that supplications, prayers, intercessions, and thanksgivings be made for all men (1 Timothy 2:1-3).*

For Ourselves: *Have no anxiety about anything, but in everything by prayer and supplication with thanksgiving let your requests be made known to God (Philippians 4:4-7).*

(Look up: Ephesians 6:18; Romans 12:11-13; 1 John 5:13-15).

PRAYER OF FAITH

When we pray to God we need to pray with the confidence that God exists and rewards those who seek Him. We should have the confidence that God hears our prayer and in His own way is working out the situation and people for whom we pray. Jesus told us that when we pray we should pray believing that we will receive the things for which we pray.

(Look up: Mark 11:23-24; Matthew 21:20-22).

PRAYER OF LISTENING

Prayer not only includes our speaking to God but also God speaking to us. God desires to share His life and Kingdom with us. He desires to speak to us, directing our lives and leading us in the things that He wants us to do. There are a number of different ways in which God speaks to us.

- *Quietness:* in order for us to hear what God wants to say to us, we need to cultivate (develop) the habit of listening to Him. Some of our time in prayer should be spent in quietness and silence. If we are always talking, then we do not give God much opportunity to speak to us.

- *God Speaks Through Other People:* God makes known His desires and expectations of us quite often through other people, especially through our Priests and Pastors, as well as other Christian people. God also speaks to us through the direction and advice of our Parents. When we go to Church we should expect God to speak to us though the Sermon, the Bible, the Readings and Prayers. In the Old Testament God often spoke through the prophets to tell His people what He wanted them to do. In the same manner God uses His Priests, Pastors and other Christian People to make known what He wants to say to His People today.[15]

- **God Speaks to Us through the Bible:** the Bible is one of God's chief ways in which He speaks to his People and to us. Through the Bible we learn more about the nature of God; what He has promised to us because we are His children; and also what He wants us to do.

In the Second Book of Kings chapters 22-23; we find the story of King Josiah, the King of Israel. During His reign they were counting the money in the Treasury of the Temple (Church) when one of the priests found a very, very old Book. When he examined it he realized that it was a copy of the "Book of the Law" which had been lost for centuries. In this Book were written directions on how God's People should live, act and worship God. When the King read the Book he called all the People of Israel together and told them what was written in the Book and how they would all have to make some big changes in the way they lived and in the way they worshipped God. This was because the "Book of the Law" showed them that what they had been doing and the way that they had been worshipping God was very wrong and because of this God

---

[15] Different Christian traditions use different titles to refer to their ordained clergy. These include minister, pastor and priest. Minister is the usual term for a clergy person in the evangelical tradition, whereas priest is more akin to the catholic and Anglo-Catholic traditions. The word Pastor is used by Pentecostal churches as well as some Catholic churches.

was very angry with them. Immediately the people began to change the things they did and the way in which they worshipped and they began to do all that the "Book of the Law" told them to do. This story is an example of how easy it is to do wrong things and even to worship God in the wrong way. Just as the People of Israel began to do what was written in the "Book of the Law," so must we do what is written in the Bible.

- ***God Speaks To Us Through The Holy Spirit***: as Christian people we have God the Holy Spirit living and dwelling in our hearts. From within us He teaches us and directs us in the things we ought to do. He does this by sharpening the voice of our consciences that warn us when we are going to do the wrong thing. From within us the Holy Spirit also speaks to our minds, showing us what God wants us to do. He does this through a small still voice. He never shouts at us, nor does He condemn us, but He gently speaks to us and helps us in our decisions and actions. Even when we do something wrong He never condemns us but gently shows us what we have done wrong and how to make it right again.

To hear God speak to us we need to be ready to listen to Him and heed what He says to us (Look up the story of Elijah in 1 Kings 19:9-18; John 16:1-15).

DISCUSSION QUESTIONS: PRAYER

1. List any words that you have not understood.
2. What is prayer?
3. What does thanksgiving involve?
4. When do we need to give thanks to God more than ever?

5. What are the two types of sacrifice that originates entirely from ourselves?

6. What does God inhabit?

7. What does rebellion do?

8. Who is responsible for the things we do?

9. What does God do when we admit and confess our sins to Him?

10. What happens to our Christian lives if we do not forgive people that have done wrong to us or hurt us?

11. Complete this sentence: "..AS HE HAS FORGIVEN US."

12. Our relationship with God grows and strengthens as we continue to do what?

13. What should we do if our relationship with God has grown cold and distant?

14. What does the word intercession mean?

15. Who should we pray for daily?

16. What do the words supplication and petition mean?

17. Why is quietness an important part of prayer?

18. Who are some of the people that God uses to speak to us?

19. What do we learn from God when we read the Bible?

20. Where does the Holy Spirit live and dwell?

21. What does the Holy Spirit do to our consciences?

22. With what type of voice does the Holy Spirit speak to our minds?

23. What should you do when you first arrive at Church and again just before you leave?

CHAPTER SEVEN
CHRISTIAN MEDITATION

Jewish-Christian meditation has existed for thousands of years. We find the first reference to meditation in the time of Abraham, where we see Abraham's son, Isaac, going out into the fields to meditate (Genesis 24:63). Our next reference comes in the time of Joshua, the son of Nun. Moses had just died and Joshua had taken his place as leader of Israel. It was Joshua's job to take the people of Israel into the Promised Land. God told Joshua that He would be with him wherever he went. God also commanded Joshua to meditate day and night on all that was contained in the Book of the Law. God promised Joshua that he would prosper and be successful in all that he did if he continued to meditate upon and do all that was contained in the Book of the Law (Joshua 1:5-9). Other references in the Old Testament to meditation can be found in Psalms: 1, 9, 49, 63, 77, 104, 119, 143, and 145.

WHAT IS MEDITATION?

Meditation is an activity. It is the activity of thinking about, pondering upon, investigating and dwelling upon the things of God. Christian Meditation focuses upon the nature of God and our Lord Jesus Christ, as well as upon the Bible and all it contains about God and the things of His Kingdom. Christian Meditation is an active and alert state of mind and spirit. It is thus quite different from other types of meditation that require a passive or inactive state of mind (as used in Eastern Meditation and Transcendental Meditation).

Not only is Christian Meditation concerned with thinking about the things of God, it also involves acting upon what we learn from this process of meditation. This is emphasised by the meaning of the Greek world *"Meleta"* which means not only *'to meditate'* or *'to think about'*, but also *'to do'* or *'to practice'*. It is for this reason that the Revised Standard Version of the Bible translates 1 Timothy 4:15 as, "practice these duties", whereas the Authorized Version of the Bible translates it as, "meditate upon these things". Christian Meditation also brings the meditator into a receptive attitude to receive from God and to understand His ways, and it does this without disengaging either the mind or the will.

Christian Meditation takes us into a much deeper level of thinking than we go normally. Such meditation bears good fruit in the lives of those who use it. It not only leads the meditator into a deeper understanding and knowledge of his or her faith and God, but also it allows the Word of God to become part of his or her very make-up and nature. It becomes what James calls "the implanted (or engrafted) word which is able to save your souls" (James 1:21); and what John calls, "the word of God abides (dwells) in you" (1 John 2:14). Christian Meditation also helps in what Paul calls the renewing of our minds. He wrote, "Do not be conformed to this world, but be transformed by the renewal of your minds, that you may prove what is the will of God, what is good and acceptable and perfect" (Romans 12:2).

THE RESULTS OF MEDITATION

Meditation touches the core of our hearts and helps to instruct our souls in the things we should do and believe as we live in and through Jesus Christ. Therefore Meditation impacts us in a number of ways including:

a) Prosperity and Success

Meditation is the means to a prosperous and successful life. Because, as a result of his meditation, the meditator lives his life according to God's Will and direction, he reaps the harvest of all the good things God wants to give to us. Meditation not only requires thinking about the things of God but doing what God requires. If we will daily meditate upon the Word of God and do what it tells us to do, then we will prosper in the things we do (Read Joshua 1:8; and Psalm 1:1-3).

b) We Will Have Health

Meditation helps to produce a healthy emotional state as well as influencing our minds and hearts. Meditation helps in the times of emotional crisis and trouble. It strengthens our will's ability to discern and choose the right course of action, setting us free from bondages that would keep us from obeying God and the admonitions (warnings) of our consciences. The Psalmist writes, "My soul is feasted as with marrow and fat... when I think of thee (God) upon my bed and meditate on thee in the watches of the night" (Psalm 63:5-6).

c) Help In The Time of Trouble and Depression

Meditation helps in the time of trouble, sorrow, grief, despair, and depression. It takes us from a place of despair and hopelessness to a place of calmness and peace. It helps us to take our minds from the situation at hand and place them once again on God and His ability to help us in our time of sorrow. God shows us that meditation can lead us from negative thoughts of depression and despair to positive thoughts of peace and calmness, and then to a place of trust and oneness with Him. He shows us how meditation can help to overcome the stunning effect of our fears and anxieties and helps us rely upon God's strength and power in the times of trouble.

WHAT TO MEDITATE ON

The greatest aid to Christian Meditation is to meditate upon the scriptures (the Bible). The Bible tells us about God and the things He does; it tells us what God has promised to us as His

Children; and it tells us how to live and act as Christian People. Paul tells us that, "All scripture is inspired by God and profitable for teaching, for reproof, for correction, and for training in righteousness, that the man of God may be complete, equipped for every good work" (2 Timothy 3:16-17).

It is important to begin small, taking a small portion of the Bible, a verse or two, and begin to use this to meditate upon. We can take one of the thousands of promises for us found in the Bible or a verse that relates to a particular need or problem in our lives. Some examples of these are:

Promises:

- The promise of eternal life (John 6:47, 8:51; 8:51, 11:25-26; 1 John 5:11).

- The promise that all things are possible to those who believe (Mark 9:23).

- The promise that God will provide all our needs (Matthew 6:32-33).

- The promise that God will be with us in times of trouble (Psalm 23; Psalm 46:1-3).

Needs and Problems:

- Overcoming anxiety and worry (Philippians 4:6-7; 1 Peter 5:6-7).

- Resisting temptation (1 Corinthians 10:12-13).

- Overcoming fear (1 John 4:18; Psalm 27:1)

- Need for wisdom to make decisions (Matthew 7:7-8; James 1:5-8).

As you continue to read your Bible each day you will come across many other promises and instructions which God has given to us. When you come across a passage that particularly relates to you personally then it is helpful to underline it with a pencil and use those passages to meditate upon.

OBEDIENCE

It is not enough to just meditate or think about the things written in the Bible – to obtain the results mentioned earlier we also need to do the things that God has commanded us to do. We are to meditate upon the things of God and then to practice them. One without the other is not true Christian Meditation. Christian Meditation leads us into obedience to God and a close relationship between Him and us through Jesus Christ our Lord.

WHEN TO MEDITATE

There are a number of different times when we can meditate.

1) If we have the time, it is useful to set aside a certain amount of time each day, maybe 10 to 15 minutes. We should find ourselves a place where we can be alone and undisturbed for that time. We then spend that time thinking about and concentrating upon a small passage of scripture that interests us.

It is helpful to ask questions about the passage we are meditating upon, such as, "What is the writer saying?" and "What does this mean for me?"

2) Another way to find time to meditate is to use the spare moments of each day,

- At home – there are those frequent times during the day when we are sitting down to relax, having a cup of tea, etc. We can use these moments to turn our minds to meditation on the things of God.

- When traveling – when we are walking down the street, or traveling in the car, bus or train.

- At night – when we are lying in bed trying to go to sleep. This can be a good and peaceful time to meditate. It may even help us to go to sleep.

- In the Morning – when we arise in the morning is another good time to turn our minds to meditation for a few moments.

In order for us to use this form of meditation it is necessary for us to memorize the particular passage we want to meditate upon or to write it on a card we can carry around with us.

CONCLUSION

Some people give up on meditation after a couple of days or weeks, because they do not think it works. Meditation takes time and discipline. The fruits of meditation will take time to come, but if we continue it will bear the results that we desire and have been promised by God. Psalm 1 tells us of the person who does not walk, stand or sit in the way of evil, but delights "in the law of the LORD, and in His law he meditates day and night. 3 He will be like a tree *firmly* planted by streams of water, which yields its fruit in its season And its leaf does not wither; And in whatever he does, he prospers" (Psalm 1:2-3).

Discussion Questions: Christian Meditation

1. List any words you do not understand.

2. Meditation is the activity of..........?

3. What are the three results of meditation?

4. What do we meditate upon?

5. How is meditation related to our obedience to God?

6. What are the two different time periods that we can use for meditation?

7. Write out on a piece of card either of the following passages:

1 Peter 5:5-7; or Philippians 4:6-7. Use one of the two types of time periods to meditate on one of these two passages. Do this for one week.

Chapter Eight

Faith

Let us also lay aside every weight, and sin which clings so closely, and let us run with perseverance the race that is set before us, looking to Jesus the pioneer and perfector of our faith (Hebrews 12:1-2).

God the Focus of Our Faith

God Himself is always the focus of faith. The reason we often lose our faith, or dwell in unbelief, is because we have taken our eyes and hearts off God. Whenever we use words such as "impossible", "doubt", "unable", "cannot" we have taken our eyes off God and His ability to do something. We look only upon ourselves and the negative situations we face. While we concentrate on self and the impossibility of our situation, we will continue to be tossed to and fro by unbelief and doubt. The first step towards faith must always be a step towards God. We need to lift our eyes and hearts off ourselves and onto Him who can do all things.

Men of Little Faith

The Gospel stories tell us that Jesus often upbraided (reproached) His disciples because of their "little faith." On one occasion, Jesus was walking across the sea, intending to pass by the disciples unseen. However, when Peter saw Him and recognized Him, Peter climbed out of the boat and began to walk across the top of the water to Jesus. When he had almost reached Jesus, his focus moved off Jesus and onto the wind and the waves around him, and he sank into the water. When he cried out for help, Jesus reached down and took Peter's hand and lifted him up on top of the water again and said to him, "O man of little faith, why did you doubt?" (Read the story in Matthew 14:22-23).

Jesus chastised Peter for his little faith. On other occasions He chastised His disciples for their little faith. He did this when they doubted God's provision of their everyday needs, such as food and clothing (Matthew 6:30-31; 16:7-8); and again when they had failed to heal a young boy who was an epileptic and who was possessed by an unclean demon (Matthew 17:14-21). Jesus' chastisement of His disciple's lack of faith was not aimed at belittling them, but to make them aware of their need to grow in the area of faith. When they had failed to heal the young boy, Jesus said to them: "O faithless and perverse generation, how long am I to be with you? How long am I to bear with you? Bring him here to me" (Mat 17:17).

The statement "perverse generation" was not meant to call them names. They had grown up in an environment where the religious traditions had become perverted.[16] Unless they broke out of the mindset of their generation they would never see God do the miracles through them that they had seen Jesus do. Likewise, unless we break out of the rationalistic and human-istic mindsets of our own generation we will not see the miracle working power of God active in our own lives and in the lives of others through us. We need to have faith.

MUSTARD SEED FAITH

However, the amount of real faith we need to have is very small indeed! The criticism of His disciples was not aimed simply at their lack of faith, but also because they did not use the faith they did have. Jesus said to His disciples, "For truly, I say to you, if you have the faith as a grain of mustard seed, you will say to this mountain, 'Move from here to there', and it will

---

[16] The Greek words used for perverted generation actually mean, "having been perverted generation."

move; and nothing will be impossible to you" (Matthew 17:20; see also Matthew 21:21-22; Mark 11:22-23; and Luke 17:5-6). All the faith we need to do anything for God and with God needs only to be the size of a mustard seed and that is quite small indeed. Paul tells us that we have all been given a measure of faith and we are called to use the measure of faith that we have been given (Romans 12:3). Our problem is that we often seem to be so encompassed about with unbelief and so overwhelmed with doubt that we fail to use the faith we do have. We need to turn our eyes away from our doubt and unbelief and turn them back to God and begin to use the small amount of faith that dwells in our hearts, the faith the size of a mustard seed. That is all the faith we need.

WITHOUT FAITH WE CANNOT PLEASE GOD

Without faith we cannot please God. The Scripture notes: "and without faith it is impossible to please him (God). For whoever would draw near to God must believe that he exists and that he rewards those who seek him" (Hebrews 11:6). Everything we do as Christians involves faith. Paul writes, "I have been crucified with Christ; it is no longer I who live, but Christ who lives in me; and the life I now live in the flesh I live by faith in the son of God who loved me and gave himself for me" (Galatians 2:20). Paul tells us that he lives his life in this world by faith in our Lord Jesus Christ. Our whole life is to be lived by faith. We should live our lives with a reliance and dependence upon the Son of God who gave Himself upon the cross for us. When the people asked Jesus what they needed to do to be doing the "works" of God, He replied to them, "this is the work of God that you believe in him whom he has sent." (John 6:29). That is, we are to believe in the one whom God had sent, Jesus Christ His Son. Everything we do as Christians should be focused upon God and begin with our belief and faith in Jesus Christ, the one whom God has sent (see Acts 15:9).

81

FAITH AND GOOD WORKS

The relationship between faith and good works is very clear in the New Testament. Without faith no amount of good works or good deeds will save you. It is not enough to be a good person. Without faith all the effort in the world will be futile. We are saved by our belief and faith in Jesus Christ and what He has done for us. Our own efforts to be good or perfect are of little value. Our salvation depends upon Him who was sent into the world to save His people from their sins. It all depends upon Jesus Christ (Matthew 1:21; 1 John 3:5). Paul writes, "for grace you have been saved through faith; and this is not your own doing, it is the gift of God – not because of works, lest any man should boast" (Ephesians 2:8-9). And again, in Romans Paul writes, "if you confess with your lips that Jesus is Lord and believe in your heart that God raised him from the dead, you will be saved. For man believes with his heart and so is justified (made right with God), and he confesses with his lips and so is saved" (Romans 10:9-10).

At the same time, if we do have true faith in Jesus Christ then this faith will produce good works and deeds. Paul completes his statement about faith with these words, "for we are his workmanship, created in Christ Jesus for good works, which God prepared beforehand, that we should walk in them" (Ephesians 2:10). We are saved by faith in order that we might walk in good works. Good works by themselves will not save us, but saving faith will produce good works. James also makes this clear when he tells us that just because someone says they have faith, it does not mean that they have true faith. Unless his faith is also supplemented and completed by good works and deeds then it is not real faith. Faith without works is dead says James. God works and deeds complete real faith (see James 2:14-26).

HOW TO INCREASE OUR FAITH

Faith always requires action. With most of the promises of God there are accompanying conditions that we must carry out in order for God to fulfill His promise to us. For instance, God promises that if we give, then it will be given back to us in the same measure we give. Also if we die to ourselves and live to God then we will be given new and abundant life. Not only that but if we will forgive others then we will be forgiven. No amount of the stirred up kind of faith or belief will substitute for obedience to God and what He commands us to do. Faith will bring us to a place of obedience. We are called to obey God and that obedience will open up a new growth in our faith.

Another way in which we can increase our faith is to study and learn what God has said in His Word, the Bible. Paul writes, "faith comes by hearing, and hearing by the Word of God." (Romans 10:17 Authorized Version). God's Word sparks new faith in our hearts and unleashes our ability to believe God for what He has promised. Quite often we lack faith purely because of ignorance, because we do not know what God has said or promised to us. If we want our faith to grow and be strong then we must seriously study and reflect upon God's Word. We need to continually read and study the Bible, so that we might know what God has promised us and what He has commanded us to do. Paul writes, "All scripture is inspired by God and profitable for teaching, for reproof, for correction, and for training in righteousness, that the man of God may be complete, equipped for every good work" (2 Timothy 3:15-17). James also writes, "therefore put away all filthiness and rank growth of wickedness and receive with meekness the implanted word, which is able to save your soul" (James 1:21).

SEED FAITH

A further help to our faith is a process that is called "seed faith". This revolves around the principle that: what you sow you will reap. Paul states this principle in the following way, "do not be deceived; God is not mocked, for whatever a man sows, that he will also reap. For he who sows to his own flesh will from the flesh reap corruption; but he who sows to the Spirit will from the Spirit reap eternal life" (Galatians 6:7-8). Jesus also spoke of sowing and reaping and mentions quite a number of different spiritual and physical seeds that we can sow to reap the fruits of eternal and spiritual life, as well as the prosperity that God promises to us as His children. Some of these are:

SEED TO SOW

- Forgive others
- Give to God and others
- Die to our selfishness
- Humble ourselves
- Do not judge others

HARVEST TO BE REAPED

- And God will forgive you (Matthew 6:14-15; Luke 6:37)
- Give, and it will be given to you; good measure, pressed down, shaken together, running over, will be put into your lap. For the measure you give will be the measure you get back" (Luke 6:36).
- And you will reap eternal life (John 12:24-26; Matthew 10:39).
- And God will exalt you (1 Peter 5:6; James 4:6, 10).
- And you will not be judged (Luke 6:37).

These are only a few of the many seeds the Bible tells us to sow to reap the benefits of God's life and kingdom. We all sow seeds every day of our lives. Some of these seeds are negative and others are positive. To grow in faith we need to sow the right type of seeds to reap a harvest of righteousness, spiritual life and prosperity as well as eternal life in God's Kingdom.

STEPS OF SEED FAITH:

1. God is the Source of all you need

2. Sow your seed, give that it may come back multiplied.

3. Pray over your sown seed. Prayer is like water that helps the crops to grow.

4. Expect to reap a harvest. Expect God to do a miracle for you.

5. Give thanks to God for the harvest He has given to you. Thank God for the miracle He has done for you.[17]

---

[17] Oral Roberts, *Miracle of Seed-Faith* (New Jersey: Spire books, Fleming H. Revell, 1970). chapter 2.

DISCUSSION QUESTIONS: FAITH

1. Who must be the focus of our faith?

2. What must our first step always be towards faith?

3. What did Jesus continually upbraid His disciples about?

4. What size of faith do we need to do anything for God?

5. What does Paul tell us we have all been given?

6. What do we need to turn our eyes away from?

7. What is our whole life to be lived by?

8. What did Jesus say we needed to do, to be doing the works of God?

9. What are we saved by?

10. What does true faith produce?

11. What is dead without faith?

12. What does faith always required?

13. What two things will bring a new growth or increase in our faith?

14. What will a man reap?

15. Write out the four steps of Seed Faith.

CHAPTER NINE

HEALING

PRAYER FOR HEALING

You cannot read very far into the Gospel Stories about Jesus without realizing that a majority of the ministry and teaching of Jesus related to healing the sick. Not only did Jesus heal those who had spiritual and emotional problems, He also healed those who were physically ill. Most of the healing stories in the Gospels related to Jesus healing those who were physically sick. Jesus healed all those who were brought to Him for help, and He healed them through prayer and the healing power of God (Matthew 4:23; 9:35; Mark 1:32-34; Luke 5:17; 6:19; 8:46).

Even while Jesus was with His disciples, they shared with Him in this ministry of healing. Jesus on a number of occasions sent them forth in pairs to "heal the sick, raise the dead, cleanse lepers, cast out demons" (Matthew 10:8; Luke 10:1,9). After Jesus ascended to the right hand of the Father in heaven, His disciples continued His ministry of healing the sick. They continued to pray for the sick and heal them through the power of God (Acts 4:30; 5:12-16; 9:32-34). This ministry of healing has continued in the Church down through the centuries to today. The same power of God that worked through Jesus and His disciples, works today through God's Priests, Pastors and other Christian People to heal the sick.

TYPES OF HEALING

There are five basic areas in our lives where we can become sick or ill. Each area needs a different type of ministry and prayer for healing.

1. Spiritual Illness

This type of illness lies at the very core of our being and lives. It affects our whole life and can affect our emotional and physical well-being as well. This illness is caused by our sin and rebellion against God and our disobedience to His commands and counsel for our lives. Healing occurs when we repent, confess our sins to God and make restitution for the things we have done. The prayer of absolution from a priest or pastor is effective in bringing healing to this part of our lives (John 20:23).

2. Emotional Illness

This type of illness is caused by the traumatic experiences we have had in the past. This includes experiences of grief, rejection, accidents and many other things that have happened to us which leave scars upon our personalities and affect our emotional well-being. Tensions, stress and pressure in our daily lives can also affect our emotions and personalities as we more and more feel that we can no longer cope with the everyday pressures that we face. Problems with fear, anxiety, anger, despair, dejection, cynicism and many others are related to emotional illness.

The healing of this type of illness occurs through the ministry of "Prayer for Inner Healing" or the "Healing of the Memories". This ministry can take place over a long period of time depending on the complexity of the problems involved and the depth of the hurts that have occurred. Often the healing is instantaneous. In this ministry we ask Jesus to go back and heal the hurts of the past, especially those related to the emotional illness that has occurred.[18]

---

[18] See: Andrew Peters, *Healing from God* (Ballan, Victoria: A.E. & L.A. Peters Outreach Enterprises, 1985).

Many people do not seek help for the emotional illnesses that they might have because they think there is something wrong with them if they have emotional problems. Emotional illness is no different from physical illness, it simply means that a different part of our being is affected and needs to be cared for and healed. We should not be hesitant to seek help from our priests, pastors and other qualified people when we feel that we have emotional problems, for they indeed may be able to help us and relieve us of the problems we are going through.

3. Physical Illness

This type of illness is caused in many ways, through germs, diseases, accidents and other physical causes. There are also many physical illnesses that people have from birth. The healing of this type of illness occurs through the "Prayer of Faith" where we pray and ask God to heal the particular illness. Some physical illnesses are caused by emotional illness and once the emotional illness has been healed the physical illness can be healed as well.

4. Broken Relationships

This type of illness occurs in families between husbands and wives, and between children and parents. It also occurs in the life of the Church and in the life of our society where we see bitter and broken friendships and hostility between neighbors and countries. Racism, elitism, cliques, divorces, and runaway children are all symptoms of this type of illness. This type of illness more often than not is a development of resentment and bitterness that has shattered close relationships and friend-ships. When God heals relationships He does a number of things. First He heals the individual persons in the relationship and then through the prayer of forgiveness He heals the relationship itself. In these situations God gives a new spark of love and affection to the relationships.

5. Oppression of the Devil

When we talk about this type of illness it is important to note the difference between "possession and "oppression". Very few people are ever possessed by the devil whereby he has full control of their lives. On the other hand, demonic or evil spirits oppress many people in various areas of their lives. Another word for oppression would be "harassment." Healing occurs through the ministry of "deliverance" or "exorcism". First the door must be closed to the influence of demonic spirits by confession and then by renouncing the devil and all his works. This involves renouncing any particular sin that has been committed or any involvement in the occult. After this is done, prayer in the name of Jesus will release the person from the harassment of the demonic spirits when they are commanded to leave the person being harassed.

THE MINISTRY OF HEALING

The ministry of healing has continued in the life of the Church since the time of Jesus Himself. James writes, "Is any among you sick? Let him call for the elders of the Church, and let them pray over him, anointing him with oil in the name of the Lord; and the prayer of faith will save the sick man, and the Lord will raise him up; and if he has committed sins, he will be forgiven. Therefore, confess your sins to one another, and pray for one another, that you may be healed" (James 5:14-16). When we become sick we should not only ring up our doctor but also our priest (elder) or pastor, and ask him to come and anoint us with oil and pray for us to be healed, and made entirely whole in every part of our being.

The Church's ministry of healing does not conflict with the work of doctors, nurses and medicine, but together they work to bring healing and wellness to those who are sick.

DISCUSSION QUESTIONS: HEALING

1. Through what did Jesus heal people?

2. What did the disciples continue after Jesus ascended into heaven?

3. How is spiritual illness healed?

4. What do priests or pastors do that is effective in healing spiritual illness?

5. What are the two names of the type of healing used to heal emotional illnesses?

6. What is the name of the type of healing used to heal physical illnesses?

7. What does God do to heal broken relationships?

8. What does James tell the sick person to do?

9. Who in addition to a doctor, do we call when we are sick?

CHAPTER TEN

DISCIPLESHIP

The basic call of the Christian Gospel is for all men, women and children to become "disciples" of our Lord Jesus Christ. Just before Jesus ascended up into heaven he left this command with His disciples, "go therefore and make disciples of all nations" (Matthew 28:18). They were called not only to bring people into the fellowship of the Church, but also to make them "disciples". This message and call to discipleship was made to all people without exception. It means that every one of us has been called to be a "disciple" of Jesus Christ.

TO FOLLOW JESUS

The disciples of Jesus were initially called to follow Him. Whenever Jesus called someone to follow Him, He never promised any benefits. He never promised that they would live forever or that they would have riches and prosperity, or even that they would have peace and tranquility. The initial call was always primarily a call to follow Jesus Himself because of who He was and not because of the fringe benefits. Jesus was God come in human form, the one and only true Messiah, the one and only true way to God the Father. In fact the call to follow Jesus was enough to threaten the future, to threaten life, to threaten prosperity, and to threaten peace and tranquility. The call to follow Jesus always meant a call to be willing to forgo and forsake the things of this world. For Peter, Andrew, John and James it meant leaving the family fishing business and following this stranger from Nazareth in Galilee. For Matthew the tax collector it meant leaving his profession and following this new stranger in town (Matthew 4:18-22; 9:9).

The call to follow often meant an incredible decision, the cost of respect and reputation, the cost of friends and loved ones.

Luke records for us the story of three men who told Jesus that they desired to follow Him. To the first man Jesus warned him that it might mean a life of destitution, starvation and exile. To the second man, who wanted first to go back and bury his father who had just died, Jesus said, "leave the dead to bury their own dead; but as for you, go and proclaim the kingdom of God." And to the third man, who wanted first to go and say farewell to his family and friends, Jesus said, "no one who puts his hand to the plow (plough) and looks back is fit for the kingdom of God" (Luke 9:57-62). The call to follow Jesus stood over and above everything. Jesus allowed no one to place anything before this call to follow Him. This includes riches, family, friends, recreation, career and work. Even the saving of our own lives is not to be more important than His call to follow. His call was greater than all these things because of who He was, the Son of God calling a wayward people back to God (see Luke 9:23-27; 18:18-30; John 12:26).

The call to follow Jesus will never leave us where it found us. Whether our answer is "Yes" or "No", our life will never be the same again. The call of Jesus to follow Him is devastating in its effect. It is important in our Christian lives that this issue is clear. When Jesus calls us to follow Him, it is because of whom He is that He makes that call. If we are only attracted to Him because of a desire for the fringe benefits, then our experience of God will be an up and down thing, tossed to and fro by whatever circumstances into which we are thrown. If we have not responded to follow Jesus over and above everything, then we will find it easy to be swayed by the things that happen to us. The call to follow Jesus will always cost us everything.

WE ARE NOT OUR OWN

A disciple of Jesus Christ no longer belongs to himself. Paul writes, "do you not know that your body is a temple of the Holy Spirit within you, which you have from God? You are not your own; you were bought with a price. So glorify God in your body" (1 Corinthians 6:19-20). As disciples of Jesus Christ everything we have including ourselves belongs to God. We no longer own anything nor should we think of anything as being our own but God's. In fact, whether or not we believe in God and serve Him, our lives and everything we own, already belongs to God because He made us what we are.

THE LORDSHIP OF JESUS CHRIST

A disciple of Jesus is one who has accepted Jesus Christ as Lord. Paul writes, "if you confess with your lips that Jesus is Lord and believe in your heart that God raised Him from the dead, you will be saved. For man believes with his heart and so is justified, and he confesses with his lips and so is saved" (Romans 10:9-10). The confession of our lips that brings us the salvation of God is, "Jesus is Lord". By this Paul means that Jesus is our Lord. HE is the one to whom we have given our lives and He is the one who we have committed ourselves to obey and serve. The Lordship of Jesus means that He is the one who calls the shots, he is the one who commands and we are the ones who obey.

If Jesus is our Lord then there will be a willingness in our lives and actions to do what He wants us to do. If Jesus is Lord, then there will be a desire within us to seek out His purpose and goals for our world, community and church, and a desire to help Him fulfill that purpose and goals. If Jesus is our Lord then we will constantly seek His counsel and direction for our lives and we will be open to hear what He wants to say to us. If Jesus is not our Lord then we are not saved, and our lives are built upon sand that one day will cave in, instead of being built on sturdy rock, the Rock that will last forever, Jesus Christ the Lord (Matthew 6:33; 7:24-29).

THE CROSS

A disciple of Jesus Christ is one who has met the Cross. The Cross of our Lord Jesus Christ has burned its mark upon our hearts putting to death our old man of selfishness and rebellion. Through the Cross we have met with death, death to our old selves filled with wickedness and corruption. Through the Cross we have died to ourselves, to our egos, to our desires and goals. In the place of the old self there arises a new person whose heart is turned to God to obey Him and to do what is right. Paul writes, "I have been crucified with Christ: it is no longer I who live but Christ who lives in me; and the life I now live in the flesh I live by faith in the Son of God, who loved me and gave Himself for me" (Galatians 2:20). Disciples of Jesus Christ are people who no longer live for themselves, but people who live for God, allowing the life of Jesus to live in them to the extent that they can say, with Paul, it is no longer I who live but Christ who lives in me. A disciple of Jesus Christ is a new person, the old self or person has passed away and behold an entirely new person has begun. Paul writes, "therefore, if anyone is in Christ, he is a new creation; the old has passed away, behold the new has come" (2 Corinthians 5:17).

Jesus spoke of the cross in another way as well. He often told his disciples to take up their cross and follow Him. The cross was always a sign of death, a sign that the disciples of Jesus knew very well, for they had seen thousands of their countrymen crucified by the Romans before their very eyes. To be worthy to be a disciple of Jesus Christ they had to be willing to lose everything, even their own lives. Jesus told them if they loved anything more than Him; their families, their careers, their ambitions, the comfort of their own homes, then they were not worthy to be called His disciples (Matthew 10:34-39).

However, when Jesus called His disciples to take up their cross and follow Him, it was always because there was something greater at stake. There was something present before them that was far greater and more powerful and far more glorious than anything they had ever known, Jesus Himself, the King of Kings and the Lord of Lords. And always on these occasions Jesus promised that those who lost their lives on account of Him would inherit eternal life and those who had given up families, homes, and careers on His account would receive it back a hundredfold (Matthew 16:24-28; 19:23-30). Disciples of Jesus Christ are people who have met the Cross!

"L" PLATES

Disciples of Jesus Christ are learners. The word disciple means student or pupil. No matter how long we have been Christians, nor how mature we are, we are still learners. A disciple never stops learning more and more about God and His ways. The disciples of Jesus had spent nearly three and a half years with Jesus in an intensive training and teaching course and at the end of that time Jesus said to them, "I have yet many things to say to you, but you cannot bear them now. When the Spirit of truth comes, he will guide you into all truth" (John 16:12-13). If after three and a half years with Jesus personally, they had not learnt it all, then it will take a long time before we have learnt it all. A disciple of Jesus Christ is one who studies God's Word, the Bible, who continually seeks His will and who listens to His counsel and direction for his or her life.

DISCUSSION QUESTIONS: DISCIPLESHIP

1. What is the basic call of the Christian Gospel to all men, women and children?

2. What was the initial call Jesus always gave to people?

3. What might the call to follow Jesus cost us?

4. As Christians do we own ourselves? Who do you think owns us?

5. What is the confession of our lips that brings us the salvation of God?

6. What does it mean for Jesus to be our Lord?

7. Through the Cross what have we met?

8. Through the Cross what do we die to?

9. Who do disciples of Jesus Christ live for?

10. What does the word disciple mean?

11. What does a disciple of Jesus Christ study?

12. Who does the disciple listen to for counsel and direction in his life?

CHAPTER ELEVEN
GIVING AND TITHING

MAMMON'S RULE

During His ministry Jesus had a lot to say about the place of money and material possessions in our lives. Material possessions are not bad in themselves, but the place those possessions have in our lives can be bad. Jesus told us that we cannot serve two masters; we cannot serve God and Mammon (money and riches). Jesus said, "No one can serve two masters; for either he will hate the one and love the other, or he will be devoted to the one and despise the other. You cannot serve God and mammon" (Matthew 6:24). Jesus warns us to make sure that money and the desire for material possessions doesn't become the consuming passion of our lives. If mammon rules our lives and ambitions then it can very easily lead us away from God and His purposes for our lives. Mammon's influence in our lives can be so strong that it can lead us into conflict with God's purposes for our lives and for the life of His Church.

Jesus goes on to tell us that wherever our treasure is that is where our heart will be as well. He says, "do not lay up for yourselves treasures on earth, where moth and rust consume and where thieves break in and steal, but lay up for yourselves treasure in heaven, where neither moth nor rust consumes and where thieves do not break in and steal. For where your treasure is, there will your heart be also" (Matthew 6:19-21). It is important for us to note the transitory (merely temporary) nature of our life in this world. We should seek treasure in heaven that will last forever, rather than the temporary nature of the silver and gold of this world.

Jesus does not ignore our need for security and material provisions. He does, however, warn us that these needs should not be the first priority of our lives. He said "but seek first his (God) kingdom and his (God) righteousness, and all these things shall be yours as well" (Matthew 6:33). The things that Jesus promises here to be ours are the things that we need to live and survive in this world, such as food, clothing, work and a home in which to live. If we will seek God first, then He will provide all we need to live in this world.

THE PRINCIPLE OF GIVING

Jesus gives us the secret of giving and prosperity when He said, "give, and it will be given you; good measure, pressed down, shaken together, running over, will be put in your lap. For the measure you give will be the measure you get back" (Luke 6:38). This promise from God takes the fear out of giving, the fear of not having enough to pay the bills and meet your needs. God promises that if we give then He will give back to us. The measure we give will be the measure we receive back. If we will give generously to God then He will give back to us generously, and God really does know how to give generously. If we give a little then we will receive a little. If we give a lot then we will receive a lot. Paul tells us that God loves a cheerful giver and that we will always have enough when we give to God and others. He writes,

> he who sows sparingly will also reap sparingly, and he who sows bountifully will also reap bountifully. Each one must do as he has made up his mind, not reluctantly or under compulsion, for God loves a cheerful giver. And God is able to provide you with every blessing in abundance, so that you may always have enough of everything and may provide in abundance for every good work" (2 Corinthians 9:6-8).

God asks us to give with expectation, the expectation that He will give back to us in proportion to what we have given to Him.

TAPPING THE RESOURCES OF GOD

Our attitude to giving will be affected by our concept of God. If we believe in a God who does not care for us and who does not become involved personally and directly in our daily lives, we will find it extremely difficult to give to God's work freely and generously. However, if we believe in the CHRISTIAN GOD, the GOD who created the universe and everything in it out of nothing; if we believe in the GOD who sent His Only Son into the world to become like us and to die for us on the cross, then the situation is very different indeed. GOD does care for us and loves us and has promised to provide everything we need to live in this world. Jesus promised that if we would seek first the kingdom of God and his righteousness, then everything we would need, clothes, food and home would be provided for us.

God's ability to provide for us is unlimited. His resources can never run out. When God promises to provide for our needs, it means that if He doesn't have it in His storehouse already then He will have it made up for us out of nothing. You cannot limit God and what he can do. Paul writes, "and my God will supply every need of yours according to his riches in glory in Christ Jesus" (Philippians 4:19). God is the source of all we need and if we will serve Him and work with Him then He will provide all we need. Too often we see the source of our needs being the wage or salary from our job, or the pocket money from Dad and Mum, or the crop we hope to harvest this year. These things are simply the instruments of God's provision for our lives. God Himself is the Source of our provision for all our needs.

THE TITHE

God has a lot to say about giving and the importance of giving for us to have a healthy and prosperous life. For nearly 3,900 years God has called His People to give to Him and His Work in this world the "tithe". The word "tithe" means "a tenth part" or "ten percent (10%)" or "one tenth". God has called His People down through the ages to give one tenth of their income to Him for the work and ministry of His Ministers and Priests (or Pastors).

THANKSGIVING

The first instance of tithing to God occurred well over 3,000 years ago with the Father of our Faith, Abraham. Abraham's nephew Lot, had been captured along with his family and all his belongings by an army led by five kings. Abraham and his men chased after then, rescued Lot, his family and recovered all his goods. On their return home they met Melchizedek, king of Salem, who brought out to them bread and wine; for he was the Priest of God Most High. Melchizedek blessed Abraham and God who had delivered him from his enemies. And then Abraham gave him a tenth of everything (Genesis 14:17-20). Abraham's giving of one tenth of everything was an act of thanksgiving to God for all that God had done for Abraham in helping him to save his nephew Lot.

THE TITHE BELONGS TO THE LORD

In Leviticus 27:30-32 we are told that all the tithe of the Lord, whether of the seed of the land or of the fruit of the trees is the Lord's and it is holy to the Lord. Also all the tithe of the herds and flocks, every tenth animal of all that pass under the herdsman's staff, shall be holy to the Lord. The tithe belongs to the Lord. The first one tenth of our income belongs to God.[19] It is not a matter of us giving a tenth of what is ours, but in fact giving to God what is His, that part of our income that belongs to God. The people were called to bring a tithe of everything, the first fruits of the grain, wine, all their income (2 Chronicles 31:2-10). As Christians we are even more aware that all that we have belongs to the Lord, so that after we have given the first ten percent of our income to the Lord through our local church, we seek Him on how He wishes us to use the other ninety percent.

THE TITHE IS GIVEN TO THE MINISTRY

The "tithe" belongs to God and God has given "His tithe" to His Priests (or Pastors) and Ministers (Leviticus 18:20-26; Nehemiah 13:10-14). When the People of Israel came into the Promised Land the land was divided into eleven sections, one section for each tribe (Manasseh and Ephraim originally being of the same tribe). However, there were originally twelve tribes. The twelfth tribe, the tribe of Levi, was set apart by God to carry out duties in the Temple of God as ministers, along with the priests of the family of Aaron (the brother of Moses). Because of this they were given no portion of land as an inheritance from God. However, in place of their portion of the land God gave them "His tithe" as an inheritance from Him. Instead of working the land like the other tribes, their work and duties were in God's Temple doing God's work. Thus the tithe was given to the Levites as God's Ministers, as an inheritance for the work they were doing for God. The Levites then tithed their income and gave it to the High Priest, Aaron, to provide for the ministry of the Priests in God's Temple. Thus the tithe of the people was given as an inheritance and income for God's Ministers and Priests. The tithe that came to them

---

[19] Normally the tithe applies to our gross income before tax is taken out of it. For businesses it is the profit before tax is taken out of it.

was the first one tenth of the income of the people (Numbers 18:24-28; 2 Chronicles 21:2-10; and Nehemiah 10:37-38; 12:44-47).

GIVING THE TITHE BRINGS A BLESSING

Not only does God call His People to give a tithe of their income for the work of His Ministers and Priests (or Pastors), He also promises that if they will give the full tithe then He will bless them both spiritually and materially. Malachi speaking for God says,

> *Bring the full tithes into the storehouse, that there may be food in my house; and thereby put me to the test, says the Lord of hosts, if I will not open the windows of heaven for you and pour down for you an overflowing blessing. I will rebuke the devourer for you, so that it will not destroy the fruits of your soil; and your vine in the field shall not fail to bear, says the Lord of hosts. Then all nations will call you blessed, for you will be a land of delight, says the Lord of hosts (Malachi 3:10-12).*

When we bring our tithes to God not only is the work of His Church provided for, but also God will pour down His blessing upon us in every area of our lives. This will not mean that we will no longer have financial problems, but it will mean that God will always provide a way for us to solve those problems.

THE TITHE IN THE NEW TESTAMENT

Jesus only directly mentions the tithe a couple of times in his teaching. Jesus seemed to consider the tithe a natural and normal thing for a godly and Christian person to be giving for the work of God's Church. Jesus refers to the tithe on two occasions when He was challenging the Pharisees about their shallow religion. The Pharisees tithed everything they produced. Jesus challenged them because, though they had been enthusiastic and boastful about their obedience to the Law in such things as tithing, they had forgotten the real essence of the Law, which was justice, mercy, faith and love. Jesus tells them that they should have been doing these things as well as not neglecting to tithe (Matthew 23:23; Luke 11:42).

Jesus makes it plain that our giving the tithe to God and his work is nothing to boast about. It is a normal part of our life with God. This is stressed in the parable of the Pharisee and Tax-Collector (Luke 18:9-14). The Pharisee thought he was pretty good because he did the right things such as tithing. He had forgotten that all that He had came from God anyway and that before God he had nothing to boast about. The tax collector on the other hand realized just what a sinner he was and how much he desperately needed God's mercy and forgiveness. The Christian is called to commit everything to God to such an extent that he no longer belongs to himself but to God (1 Corinthians 6:19-20). Everything we have belongs to God and as such we should be returning back to God at least a tithe of our income for the work and ministry of His Priests (or Pastors) and Ministers.

DISCUSSION QUESTIONS: THE PLACE OF GIVING AND TITHING

1. What is the bad thing about material possessions?

2. Jesus said we cannot serve two masters. Who are these two masters?

3. What does mammon mean?

4. What did Jesus say we should not let become a consuming passion?

5. Where does Jesus tell us to lay up treasure?

6. What should we seek first?

7. What sort of giver does Paul say God loves?

8. What will affect our attitude of giving?

9. What does the word tithe mean?

10. What kind of act was Abraham's giving of a tithe?

11. To whom does the tithe belong to?

12. To whom does God give His tithe to?

13. What does God say He will do for us if we give Him the tithe?

CHAPTER TWELVE

SHARING THE GOOD NEWS

The Good News (Gospel) of Jesus Christ is at the heart of the Church's life and purpose. Its proclamation is central to the Church's mission. Worship and proclamation of the Gospel are the two basic signs of the Church and its life. Every Christian believer is called to worship God and to proclaim and share the good news of our Lord Jesus Christ. Peter tells us concerning our call to worship:

> *Come to him, to that living stone, rejected by men but in God's sight chosen and precious; and like living stones be yourselves built into a spiritual house, to be a holy priesthood, to offer spiritual sacrifices acceptable to God through Jesus Christ (1 Pet 2:4-5).*

When it comes to proclamation he notes:

> *But you are a chosen race, a royal priesthood, a holy nation, God's own people, that you may declare the wonderful deeds of him who called you out of darkness into his marvelous light. Once you were no people but now you are God's people; once you had not received mercy but now you have received mercy (1 Pet 2:9-10).*

JESUS' CALL TO US TO PREACH THE GOSPEL

The call to share the good news comes from Jesus Himself. He instructed His disciples, and through them us, to go forth and proclaim the Gospel to the whole creation. He said, *"Go into all the world and preach the gospel to the whole creation."*[20] Evangelism means to take forth the good news of Jesus Christ and to share and proclaim it to others. One of the final

---

[20] Mark 16:15

instructions Jesus left with His disciples, after His resurrection, was:

All authority in heaven and on earth has been given to me. Go therefore and make disciples of all nations, baptizing them in the name of the Father and of the Son and of the Holy Spirit, teaching them to observe all that I have commanded you; and lo, I am with you always, to the close of the age (Mathew 28:18-20).

These words of Jesus outline for us the basic ingredients of the ministry of evangelism, which we have all been called to do by Jesus Himself. These basic ingredients are:

OUR RIGHT TO PROCLAIM THE GOSPEL

Proclaiming the Gospel is not a matter of pushing our religious viewpoint upon others. Neither is it something that we should keep private. Jesus not only instructs us to proclaim the Good News of the Kingdom of God, but He also gives us the authority to do so. He said, *"all authority in heaven and on earth has been given to me, Go therefore and make disciples of all nations."* His authority lies at the core of our responsibility and privilege, to preach and share the gospel. Jesus tells His disciples that they are to go and make disciples of all nations because He has all authority in heaven and earth. Jesus is the supreme authority in heaven and earth, and He has given us the authority to preach the Gospel to the whole creation. To share the good news with others is not forcing our own opinions upon them, but rather is sharing with them the truth about Jesus and His love for them. It is opening up for them the way to God through our Lord Jesus Christ. C.H. Spurgeon is purported to have said, Evangelism "is one beggar telling another beggar where to get the bread."[21]

---

[21] Michael Green, *Evangelsim through the Local Church* (London: Hodder & Stoughton, 1991), 8.

MAKE DISCIPLES

Jesus not only told us to proclaim the good news to others, but also to make disciples of them. It is not enough just to drag someone to church, or to bring him or her into the fellowship of our local Christian group. We are to make disciples of them. A disciple is a learner. The Greek word for disciple is *mathetes*, which literally means "pupil/learner, referring to one who learns."[22] Disciples are those who in coming to Jesus, desire to learn everything they can about loving God and following Jesus. Richard Longenecker notes that a disciple is a pupil or student who not only follows the teaching, but also the Teacher Himself. We are called to be disciples of our Lord Jesus Christ, following and obeying everything that He has taught us and also following Him.[23] Following Jesus as one of His disciples means to take his yoke upon us and to carry His burden,

Jesus said, 'Come to me, all who labor and are heavy laden, and I will give you rest. Take my yoke upon you, and learn from me; for I am gentle and lowly in heart, and you will find rest for your souls. For my yoke is easy, and my burden is light' (Matthew 11:28-30).

ALL NATIONS

The good news of our Lord Jesus Christ is for every person, in every pace, and in every time. There is no discrimination about sex, race, color or class when we come to sharing the gospel of Jesus Christ. Our Lord Jesus came to save every person, whether rich or poor, sick or well, powerful or oppressed, good

[22] R.N. Longnecker, *Patterns of Discipleship in the New Testament* (Grand Rapids, Michigan: William B. Eermans Publishing Co., 1996), 2.

[23] Longnecker, 2. Longenecker notes that the verb "to follow" (akolouthein) and the adjectival phrase "those who follow" (hoi akolouthountes) appear regularly in the Gospels referring to "disciples" as those who were committed to Jesus and followed Him.

or bad. Jesus loves all of us just as we are and He calls all men and women to Himself and through Him to God our Father. The radical thing about the teaching and preaching of Jesus was that He proclaimed the good news about the Kingdom of God, not only to the Jews, but also to the Gentiles, that is to all people regardless of their race or color. We are called to proclaim the gospel to all people.

BAPTIZING THEM

Baptism is an important part of evangelism because baptism is a sign and seal of the fundamental aspects of our being born into the kingdom of God. These aspects include:

- **Repentance**: which is a change of heart and mind about God and His ways. It is a turning from our own ways to God to love and obey Him.

- **Forgiveness:** when we come to God confessing our sins, He forgives us for all that we have done against Him and others.

- **Death:** as Christians we are called to die to our own self-centered and selfish lives and live to God.In baptism we are united with the death of our Lord Jesus upon the cross. It is this identification with the death of Christ that gives us the ability to die to ourselves and to live to God.

- **New Birth:** Jesus taught, to enter the Kingdom of God we need to have a spiritual birth. We need to be born again of the Spirit and water.

TEACHING THEM

Jesus told His disciples that they were to teach those whom they had made disciples everything that He instructed them to do. It is not enough to just bring someone to Jesus; we must also teach him, or her, the basic things about the Christian Faith. Just as a baby needs milk to grow, so also new people to the faith need spiritual milk to grow and be strengthened in their faith. We are called to teach them everything that Jesus has instructed us to do.

LO, I AM WITH YOU ALWAYS

One of the most comforting things that Jesus said to His disciples was that He would be with them. When we go forth to share the Gospel with others we are not alone. Jesus Himself goes forth with us to help us share the good news with other people. Jesus not only goes with us, He also goes before us and after us. He prepares the hearts of those to whom we speak, so they can hear what we have to proclaim and to respond to the good news of the Kingdom of God. As we share with others, Jesus Himself, through the Holy Spirit, speaks to their hearts, convicting them of the truthfulness of what we are saying and convincing them that the good news that we are sharing with them is the truth.

> Jesus said, 'Nevertheless I tell you the truth: it is to your advantage that I go away, for if I do not go away, the Counselor will not come to you; but if I go, I will send him to you. And when he comes, he will convince the world concerning sin and righteousness and judgment: concerning sin, because they do not believe in me; concerning righteousness, because I go to the Father, and you will see me no more; concerning judgment, because the ruler of this world is judged' (John 16:7-11).

In fact when we go forth to share the Gospel, Jesus does not come with us, we go with Him. In all that we do to spread the good news about Jesus we should be following Jesus and responding to the prompting and leading of the Holy Spirit. Everything that we do for God should not be done in our own power and strength, but in God's power and strength. The Holy Spirit's role is to enable us to serve and obey God the Father through our Lord Jesus Christ and to proclaim the good news of the Kingdom of God in that power. Jesus said, *"I am the vine, you are the branches. He who abides in me, and I in him, he it is that bears much fruit, for apart from me you can do nothing"* (John 15:5).

THE GOOD NEWS

The good news of Jesus Christ is the message of God's unconditional love for us. This love has been shown to us through Jesus' sacrifice for us upon the cross. *"God shows his love for us in that while we were yet sinners. Christ died for us"* (Romans 5:8). God loves us just as we are, for who and what we are as unique persons created in His own image. He loves us despite our sin and rebellion and He calls us into a love relationship with Himself.

- The Good news of Jesus Christ is the message that there is no longer condemnation for those who believe in Jesus Christ (John 3:16-18).

- It is the Good News of God's forgiveness for all that we have done against Him and others. It is the Good News of complete release and freedom from guilt and shame through God's forgiving and cleansing power flowing through our lives (1 John 1:5-10).

- It is the good news of new life in Jesus Christ: *"therefore, if anyone is in Christ, he is a new creation; the old has passed away, behold, the new has come."* (2 Corinthians 5:17).

- It is the Good News of oneness and peace with God. *"Therefore, since we are justified by faith, we have peace with God through our Lord Jesus Christ"* (Romans 5:1).

- It is the Good News of eternal life that comes through believing in Jesus Christ. Jesus said, *"I am the resurrection and the life; he who believes in me, though he die, yet shall he live, and whoever lives and believes in me shall never die"* (John 11:25-26).

- It is the Good News of the "Way" to God, the one and only way to God that is through Jesus. Jesus said, *"I am the way, the truth and the life; no one comes to the Father, but by me"* (John 14:6). And Peter said, *"and there is salvation in no one else, for there is no other name under heaven given among men by which we must be saved"* (Acts 4:12).

- It is the Good News of Jesus Himself. Christians are not called primarily to be good people, or to obey all the rules. We are called to have a personal living relationship with Jesus Christ and through Him with God the Father. We are called into a love relationship with God, the God who loves us unconditionally with a steadfast love that never wavers or varies. Through the empowering of that relationship we go forth into the world to give the same love to others that we have received from our relationship with God.

No questions this time - it is time practice what we have learnt

REFERENCE SECTION 1
THE BIBLE – THE OLD TESTAMENT

The Old Testament consists of thirty-nine (39) books written between 1700 B.C. and 100 B.C. The Old Testament was originally written in *Hebrew*. The following is the Hebrew text for Genesis 1:1

א בְּרֵאשִׁית, בָּרָא אֱלֹהִים, אֵת הַשָּׁמַיִם, וְאֵת הָאָרֶץ

1 In the beginning God created the heaven and the earth.[24]

There is also a Greek translation of the Old Testament that was written between 300 B.C. and 200 B.C. in Egypt. This version of the Old Testament is called the *Septuagint.* The following is the Septuagint Greek text for Genesis 1:1

¹εν αρχη εποιησεν ο θεοσ τον ουρανον και την γην[25]

The Old Testament tells the story of the People of God and their relationship with God. It tells how God chose the nation of Israel to be His people and of the Covenant (mutual agreement) that He established with them. It tells us the history of the Jewish people (the Israelites), of their faithfulness and unfaithfulness to the Covenant they had with God.

There are two important historical events in the history of the nation of Israel that not only affected the nation's history but

---

[24] A Hebrew - English Bible According to the Masoretic Text and the JPS 1917, Mechon Mamre HTML version, www.mechon-mamre.org/p/pt/pt0.htm

[25] Henry Sikkema, The Septuagint, the Greek Old Testament, 1999, http://spindleworks.com/septuagint/septuagint.htm

also the nature of their religious worship and life. These were the "Exodus from Egypt" when God set the people of Israel free from bondage and slavery to the Egyptians. The second event was the "Captivity in Babylon" where God allowed His People to be taken captive to the city of Babylon, because of their rebellion against Him. Even during the time when this was happening God promised that He would bring them back home in seventy years. Precisely seventy years later they came back home.

Exodus from Egypt: 1300-1220 B.C.

Captivity in Babylon: 587 B.C.

There are four different sections in the Old Testament that represent a different style of writing and material. They are:

The Law

The Historical Books

The Poetic Books

The Prophetic Books

THE LAW - *Consists of the Books:*

1. **Genesis**

2. **Exodus**

3. **Leviticus**

4. **Numbers**

5. **Deuteronomy**

These five books are called the books of the Law, or what the Jewish people call *"The Torah".* Scholars also referred to them as *"The Pentateuch".*

GENESIS

Genesis tells the story of the beginning of the universe and the creation of the world, as well as the beginning of mankind. (Genesis 1-11). It also tells the story of the beginning of the nation of Israel when God chose *Abraham* to be the Father of a new nation, a nation of God's people called *Israel.* (Genesis 12-25). It tells the story of Abraham's son Isaac and the birth of Isaac's two sons, Jacob and Esau. It is from Jacob's twelve children that the twelve tribes of the nation of Israel have their names and beginnings (Genesis 25-36). Genesis finishes with the story of Joseph, one of Jacob's sons, who became one of the chief rulers of Egypt. It explains how Jacob and his family traveled south to live in the land of Egypt (Genesis 37-50). The tribe of Israel (some 70 people – Jacob's family) lived in Egypt, and grew in numbers, for over 400 years.

EXODUS

The Book of Exodus begins with the nation of Israel still in Egypt. The nation is now much larger in number than when Jacob first took his family to Egypt. However, they are no longer citizens, but slaves to the Egyptians. It tells the story of how God set the people of Israel free from slavery through the work of Moses and his brother Aaron (Exodus 1-15). Exodus tells the story of the journey of the people of Israel through the wilderness to go to the land that God had promised Abraham and his descendants.

LEVITICUS, NUMBERS, & DEUTERONOMY

These three books continue to tell the story of the people's journey through the wilderness to the land God had promised them. It tells of their refusal to obey God's commands, at Kadesh-barnea, to go in and possess the land at its most southern border. It tells of their subsequent preparation to take the land after wandering through the wilderness for some forty years, at its most eastern border. It also relates how God gave to them laws and commandments, which included the Ten Commandments, to show them how to live and act as His People.

THE HISTORICAL BOOKS

There are twelve books that deal with the different historical periods of the history of Israel up until about 400 years before the birth of Jesus

Consists of the Books:

1. Joshua
2. Judges
3. Ruth
4. 1 & 2 Samuel
5. 1 & 2 Kings
6. 1 & 2 Chronicles
7. Ezra
8. Nehemiah
9. Esther

A/ THE PROMISED LAND

The Book of Joshua: tells the story of the nation of Israel coming into and possessing the land promised to Abraham by God. Joshua, the leader appointed by God and Moses, led them into the land of Palestine or Canaan (now called Israel).

The Book of Judges: tells the story of the early history of the nation of Israel after they had entered and dwelt in the

Promised Land. It shows their obedience and disobedience to God and the leaders (called Judges), that God had sent to set them free from their enemies.

B/ THE KINGS OF ISRAEL

The Books of 1 & 2 Samuel, as well as **1 Kings 1-11,** tell of the reign of the first three kings of Israel, Saul, David and Solomon. Saul was the first King of Israel appointed and consecrated to his position by the Prophet Samuel. David came after Saul, having defeated Goliath (the giant Philistine) in his early days, whilst still a boy. It was David who led the nation of Israel in taking and capturing the whole of the land promised to them by God. The last part of the land to be taken was the city of Jerusalem, which David then made his headquarters and the capital city of the nation. Jerusalem became the centre of the whole religious life of the people of Israel. Solomon, David's son, followed his father and is well known for his wisdom and the building of the majestic temple in Jerusalem, which stood, at least in part, from 900 B.C. to about 587 B.C. when it was sacked and robbed by the Babylonians. A number of building projects were carried out on it after the return of the Israelites from Babylon. Herod the Great carried out a complete restoration of the temple to its former glory. The temple was again destroyed in 70 A.D. and Israel as a nation disappeared for over nineteen hundred years.

C/ DIVIDED KINGDOMS

The Books of 1 Kings 12-22, 2 Kings and 1 & 2 Chronicles tell the story of the divided kingdom that occurred after the death of Solomon. The division of the kingdom occurred during the reign of Rehoboam. Immediately after Solomon's death Rehoboam increased the heavy burden of taxation and service upon the people of Israel. He did this against the good advice of the older advisers of King Solomon, who had recommended an easing of the burden upon the people. As a result the nation split into the Kingdoms of Israel and Judah.

Judah - the line of David and Solomon consisted of the two tribes of Judah and Benjamin and was called the Kingdom of Judah. Its first king was Rehoboam.

Israel - the other kingdom consisted of the ten tribes: Reuben, Simeon, Gad, Manassah/Ephraim, Zebulon, Issachar, Asher, Dan and Naphtali and was called the kingdom of Israel. The history of the divided kingdom ends with the Kingdom of Israel being destroyed and its survivors taken captive to Assyria in 721 B.C., never to return to their land again. The Kingdom of Judah was destroyed and the survivors taken captive to Babylon 587 B.C.

D/ REBUILDING THE TEMPLE AND JERUSALEM

The Books of Ezra and Nehemiah tell the story of the rebuilding of the temple in Jerusalem and the rebuilding of Jerusalem itself after the captivity in Babylon had ended. Some seventy years after the people of Judah had been taken captive to Babylon, King Cyrus of Babylon sent them back to their home in Jerusalem with enough money and goods to rebuild their temple and their homes.

THE POETICAL BOOKS

Consists of the Books:

1. **Job**
2. **Psalms**
3. **Proverbs**
4. **Ecclesiastes**
5. **Song of Songs**

These books are distinctive because of the nature of their language. They consist of the poetical writings of the nation of Israel over many hundreds of years. They consist of sayings, instructions, poetry and songs.

THE PROPHETIC BOOKS - *Consists of the Books:*

Major Prophets:

1. Isaiah
2. Jeremiah
3. Ezekiel

Minor Prophets:

4. Daniel
5. Hosea
6. Joel
7. Amos
8. Obadiah
9. Jonah
10. Micah
11. Nahum
12. Habakkuk
13. Zephaniah
14. Haggai
15. Zechariah
16. Malachi

The prophets were men sent by God to speak to the people of Israel and Judah on His behalf. God used these men to speak directly to His people so they would know what He required of them. These men were usually sent at times when the people of Israel and Judah had rebelled against God and had gone after other gods and religions. The prophets appeared in different times during the history of Israel and Judah as follows:

1. **BEFORE THE CONQUEST OF THE KINGDOM OF ISRAEL**

   In 721 B.C. the Kingdom of Israel was conquered by the nation of Assyria and the people of Israel were taken off as captives to the foreign lands of Assyria. For some eighty years before this event, from 800-721 B.C., the prophets Amos, Hosea, Micah and Isaiah foretold that this would happen. They warned the people of the Kingdom of Israel and told them to turn back to their God and worship Him only. The people did not turn back and were taken away from their land, as captives of a foreign nation.

2. **BEFORE THE CAPTIVITY IN BABYLON**

   In 587 B.C the Babylonians conquered the Kingdom of Judah and took the people of Judah away as captives to Babylon. For some 130 years before this event, from 721 - 587 B.C. the prophets Zephaniah, Nahum, Habakkuk, Jeremiah, and Isaiah foretold that this would happen. They called the people of Judah back to worship their God only. Right towards the end the people made some effort to return to God under the leadership of Josiah, but it was too little too late, and they were defeated by the Babylonians and taken away captives to Babylon.

3. **DURING THE EXILE AND CAPTIVITY IN BABYLON**

   The exile and the captivity in Babylon was to last for some seventy years and during that time God continued to speak to His people through the prophets. The prophets Ezekiel, Daniel and Obadiah joined the people in exile and spoke to them the words of God and His promise that they would be returned to their own land and to the city of Jerusalem.

4. **AFTER THE CAPTIVITY IN BABYLON**

In 516 B.C. the people of Judah (also known as Israel) returned to Jerusalem to rebuild the temple. During this time the prophets Haggai and Zechariah continued to bring God's message and words to His people. In 445 B.C. the people under the direction of Nehemiah began to rebuild the city of Jerusalem itself. During this time the last of the prophets, Malachi, continued to bring God's word to His people. Malachi was the last of the prophets to be sent by God to the nation of Israel until the time of John the Baptist and Jesus. For 400 years there was no prophet or prophetic message from God to His people.

DISCUSSION QUESTIONS: PROPHETS

We are going to look at the way God called people to do special jobs for Him. Most of these people were called prophets.

1. Read Judges 6:1-16: What did the angel of the Lord call Gideon when he first appeared to him? Who was Gideon going to defeat?

....

2. Read 1 Samuel 3:1-11: Who was really calling Samuel during the night? What did Samuel first say when he knew who was calling?

....

3. Read 2 Kings 2:1-15: What did Elisha want Elijah to do for him? What did Elisha need to "see" to receive it? Did he see it?

....

4. Read Isaiah 6:1-8: Who volunteered to do what God wanted done?

....

5. Read Jeremiah 1:1-10: What excuse did Jeremiah give to God, to not do what God wanted him to do? Did God accept his excuse?

....

TIMETABLE OF THE HISTORY OF ISRAEL

APPROXIMATE DATES

DATE

?   **THE ACCOUNT OF MAN'S ORIGINS:**

- The Creation Stories - Genesis 1-2
- Man's Disobedience - Genesis 3-5
- The Flood Story   - Genesis 6-8
- Re-creation   - Genesis 9-11
- The Tower of Babel - Genesis 11

1900-1700   **THE PATRIARCHS:**

- Abraham - Genesis 11:31-25:11
- Isaac   - Genesis 21-28
- Jacob   - Genesis 25:19-36:43

1700   **STORY OF JOSEPH:** Sojourn in Egypt - Genesis 37-50

1700-1300   **SLAVERY IN EGYPT:** 400 years captivity in Egypt - Genesis 15:12-16, Exodus 1

1300-1200   **EXODUS & JOURNEY THROUGH THE WILDERNESS**

- Exodus from Egypt - Exodus 2-14
- Journey through the wilderness - Exodus 15-18
- Mt. Sinai & Ten Commandments - Exodus 19-33

- Journey continued & further giving of laws and statutes Numbers, Leviticus & Deuteronomy

1300-1200   THE PROMISED LAND: the Book of Joshua

1200-1000   THE TIME OF THE JUDGES: Books of Judges, 1 Samuel & Ruth

1000-900   THE KINGS OF ISRAEL:

- Saul - 1 Samuel 9-31
- David - 2 Samuel, 1 Kings 1-2
- Solomon - 1 Kings 2:11-11:43

922   THE DIVIDED KINGDOM: 1Kings 12-22; 2 Kings, 1 & 2 Chronicles

- **Judah** - following the line of David, consisting of the tribes of Judah and Benjamin. Jerusalem major city and temple worship
- **Israel** - consisted of the ten tribes - Reuben, Gad, Manasseh/Ephraim, Simeon, Zebulon, Dan, Issachar, Asher and Naphtali

900-800   THE PROPHETS ELIJAH & ELISHA: 1Kings 17 – 2Kings 9

800-721   THE PROPHETS: Amos, Hosea, Micah & Isaiah

721   CONQUEST OF THE KINGDOM OF ISRAEL BY ASSYRIA: 2 Kings 17

721-587	**THE PROPHETS:** Zephaniah, Nahum, Habakkuk, Jeremiah, & Isaiah.
587	**CONQUEST OF JUDAH BY BABYLON:** Captivity in Babylon - 2 Kings 24-25
587-517	**PROPHETS IN EXILE:** Ezekiel, Daniel & Obadiah
516	**RETURN & REBUILDING OF THE TEMPLE** Esther, Ezra, Haggai and Zechariah
445	**REBUILDING OF JERUSALEM:** Nehemiah & Malachi
445-0	**HISTORY OF ISRAEL FOUND IN THE BOOKS OF THE APOCRYPHA:** These are a variety of books that cover the historical period from Malachi and the coming of John the Baptist & Jesus.

REFERENCE SECTION 2

THE BIBLE – THE NEW TESTAMENT

TEXT (WRITING)

All of the New Testament was originally written in Greek. Greek was the common language of the Roman Empire at that time. Palestine (Israel), where Jesus was teaching, was a part of the Roman Empire. The New Testament was written from 40 – 100 A.D. There are in existence today some 5,000 Greek manuscripts (copies) of the New Testament in part or whole. The following is an example of Greek from John 1:1:

1:1 εν αρχη ην ο λογοσ και ο λογοσ ην προσ τον θεον και θεοσ ην ο λογοσ

CANON OF SCRIPTURE

By the year 200 A.D. the main contents of the New Testament had been decided. At this stage the Church was still considering the letters of Hebrews, James, Jude, 2 Peter, 2 & 3 John, as well as the book of Revelation. By 390 A.D. the New Testament, in its present form, was accepted by the Councils of the Church that included all the Bishops throughout the Christian Church. The Church found it necessary to define which writings (books & letters) were authentic (real) writings because at that time the Church was plagued by a number of false writings that claimed to be Christian but were not. The test of authenticity (realness) that the Church placed upon these writings: was their origin from the twelve apostles of Jesus and also Paul. The books and letters had to either be written by an apostle or at least have his direct influence and direction. For instance, Mark was linked with Peter, and Luke with Paul.

THE NEW TESTAMENT

The New Testament includes 27 writings, consisting of the historical books such as the Gospels and the Acts of the Apostles, and also the letters to the churches.

Historical Books:

Gospel according to Matthew

Gospel according to Mark

Gospel according to Luke

Gospel according to John

The Acts of the Apostles

Letters:

Romans

1 & 2 Corinthians

Galatians

Ephesians

Philippians

Colossians

1 & 2 Thessalonians

1 & 2 Timothy

Titus

Philemon

Hebrews

James

1, 2 & 3 John

1 & 2 Peter

Jude

Revelation

THE HISTORICAL BOOKS - THE GOSPELS

The four Gospels tell the story of the life of Jesus. They tell us of His Ministry and Teaching, of His death, resurrection and ascension to the right hand of the Father in heaven.

1. **Mark** - Mark is thought to be the first of the Gospels to be written, and was written by Mark, a companion (friend) of Peter and Paul. The Gospel according to Mark was written around 60 A.D. by John Mark, who was a native of Jerusalem (Acts 12:12). He was not one of the twelve apostles of Jesus, but was with Jesus for some time and especially in the last week of Jesus' life. He was present when Jesus was arrested (the young man mentioned in Mark 14:51). He was related to Barnabas, one of St Paul's companions (Acts 13:5). Mark traveled with Paul in Asia and to Rome (Colossians 4:10; Philemon 24; 2 Timothy 4:11).

2. **Luke** - Luke the Physician wrote the Gospel according to Luke and the Acts of the Apostles. Luke was a companion of Paul. Luke was a Gentile rather than a Jew and was a medical Doctor. Luke wrote the Gospel sometime between 60 and 70 A.D. The purpose of his writing was to present a historical account of the life and ministry of Jesus and the Early Christian Church. He claims to rely on authentic (real or true) and reliable sources and material for his historical account. In this Gospel Luke upholds the cause of the underdog and poor over against the rich and powerful.

3. **Matthew** - The Apostle Matthew wrote the Gospel according to Matthew probably when he was in Jerusalem. Matthew was originally a tax collector. Jesus passed by one day and called him to follow Him and be a disciple. Matthew left his work and followed Jesus, becoming an apostle and disciple (Matthew 9:9). Matthew's other name

131

was Levi. Matthew wrote his Gospel for Jewish Christians to show that Jesus was truly the promised Messiah and Christ. He wrote around about 70 A.D.

4. **John** – Scholars propose that the Gospel according to John was written between 80 and 100 A.D. It may have been sometime earlier than that because, although John describes Jesus' foretelling of the destruction of the temple, he does not relate its actual destruction in 70 A.D. John lived to a ripe old age and was probably the last of the twelve apostles to die. He wrote the gospel in Ephesus where he spent the last few years of his life. He was the disciple whom Jesus loved (John 13:23)

Extra Note: The word "Gospel" means "Good News". Our four Gospels tell the "Good News" of God's plan of salvation for all men and women through His Son Jesus Christ.

5. ***The Acts of the Apostles*** - Luke the Physician wrote the Acts of the Apostles sometime between 60 and 70 A.D. It tells the story of the Early Christian Church after the resurrection and ascension of Jesus to the right hand of His Father in Heaven. It tells of the coming of the Holy Spirit upon the apostles and disciples of Jesus on the Day of Pentecost and the work of the Church in spreading the "Good News" about God's Kingdom and His Son Jesus Christ. It especially outlines the work of Peter and Paul.

THE LETTERS OF PAUL TO THE CHURCHES

Paul was originally a high-ranking Jew, a member of the Sanhedrin (the Jewish Council), who persecuted the Christian Church and had many of its people arrested and put to death. Paul (also called Saul) was converted to the Christian Faith about 32 A.D. when Jesus Himself appeared to him on the road to Damascus. He then became one of the Church's chief workers and preachers. Called by Jesus to be an apostle, he wrote the majority of the letters we find in the New Testament. All the letters of Paul, except for Romans, were written to Churches that Paul himself had started and built, or people he had trained in ministry.

1. **Galatians** – This is thought to be the earliest writing in the New Testament written in 48 A.D. Paul was at Antioch when he wrote this letter.

2. **Thessalonians** – Paul wrote two letters to the people of Thessalonica. He wrote them in 50 A.D. when he was in Corinth.

3. **Philippians** – This letter was written to the people of Philippi in 50 A.D. when Paul was in Corinth.

4. **Corinthians** – Paul wrote two letters to the people of Corinth. He wrote these over a period of three years from 54 to 56 A.D. He was living at that time in Ephesus and Macedonia.

5. **Romans** – Paul had not known the congregation in Rome before he wrote this letter. Two years after writing this letter, Paul was taken to Rome as a prisoner of the Roman State. He wrote this letter about 57-58 A.D. while he was at Corinth.

6. **Colossians** – Paul wrote this letter in 60 A.D. while he was a prisoner in Rome.

7. **Philemon** – This letter was also written in 60 A.D. while Paul was a prisoner in Rome.

8. **Ephesians** – Paul wrote to the people of Ephesus in 60 A.D. while he was still a prisoner in Rome.

9. **Timothy** – Paul had trained Timothy to be a minister and had placed him in charge of a number of his churches. Paul wrote these two letters to Timothy to encourage him in his

work between 63 and 64 A.D. Paul was still a prisoner in Rome when he wrote these two letters.

10. **Titus** – Titus was another minister Paul had trained and placed in charge of churches. The letter to Titus was also a letter of encouragement for the work he was doing. This letter was also written between 63 and 64 A.D., while Paul was a prisoner in Rome.

Paul spent the last years of his life in Rome where he and Peter were executed by crucifixion under the Roman persecutions around 64 A.D.

THE OTHER LETTERS TO THE CHURCH

1. *James* - James, the brother of the Lord Jesus wrote the letter of James. James was the head of the Church in Jerusalem and was martyred (executed) in 62 A.D. during the first persecution of the Christian Church by the Romans. He wrote the letter of James in 60 A.D. to Jewish Christians who were being persecuted by the Romans and who had fled to foreign countries. James emphasizes the need for a practical religion that manifested itself in good works rather than mere words.

2. *1 Peter* - Peter (Cephas) was one of the first of the apostles to be chosen by Jesus. He was an early leader in the Christian Church and much of his work is recorded in the Acts of the Apostles. In this letter Peter writes a letter of instruction to Jewish and Gentile Christians scattered throughout the area of Asia Minor. In the letter he points to the suffering and example of the Lord Jesus and calls us to follow his example and follow in his steps. The letter was written during the period 60-63 A.D. when Peter was in Rome just prior to his death by crucifixion. Sivanus wrote the letter at the dictation of Peter (Sivanus would be something like a secretary to Peter).

3. **2 Peter** - This letter claims also to be written by Peter. If so then it would have been written early in 64 A.D. Many scholars question whether this letter was actually written by Peter. They feel that it may have been written at a later date.

4. **Jude** - This letter was written by Jude the brother of James and was written between 66 and 70 A.D. Jude wrote his letter to the Christians in Syrian Antioch.

5. **Hebrews** - It is uncertain who the actual writer of this letter might be. There is some claim that it was written by Paul. The style of the letter is quite different from Paul's normal style of writing found in his other letters. However, it still contains much of Paul's ideas and concepts. It was written between 60 and 70 A.D. If it was written by Paul it would have been written around 60-64 A.D.

6. **John** - Apart from the Gospel according to John there are four other writings from the New Testament that are traditionally attributed to the Apostle John.

7. **Letters of John** - there are three letters written by John around 90 A.D. while John was living at Ephesus.

8. **Revelation** the book of Revelation was written between 69 and 96 A.D. It is thought that John the Apostle wrote this book while on the island of Patmos. This book records a vision that John experienced of heaven and of the things that were to happen in the future of our world.

DISCUSSION QUESTIONS: THE NEW TESTAMENT

List any words you did not understand.

1. In what language was the New Testament originally written?

2. In what part of the Roman Empire was Jesus teaching?

3. During what period of time was the New Testament written?

4. How many Greek manuscripts are in existence today?

5. By what year did the councils of the Church accept the New Testament in its present form?

6. What was the authenticity that the Church placed upon these writings?

7. How many writings are there in the New Testament?

8. List in order the names of the Gospels.

9. a) Who was Mark?

    b) Who was Luke?

    c) Who was Matthew?

    d) Who was John?

10. What does the word Gospel mean?

11. What is the Acts of the Apostles about?

12. Who was Paul?

13. Look up your Bible and list how many chapters there are in each of the letters of Paul?

14. Who was James?

15. Look up the two letters of Peter in your Bible and list how many chapters there are in each letter.

16. Look up the 3ʳᵈ letter of John and write down who it was written to?

17. Name the first and last books in the New Testament.

Bibliography:

Green, Michael. *Evangelsim through the Local Church.* London: Hodder & Stoughton, 1991.

Longnecker, R.N. *Patterns of Discipleship in the New Testament.* Grand Rapids, Michigan: William B. Eermans Publishing Co., 1996.

Peters, Andrew. *Healing from God.* Ballan, Victoria: A.E. & L.A. Peters Outreach Enterprises, 1985.

_____. *The Emerging Paradigm of Diversity: Its Effect on the Church and Its Leadership.* Mansfield, QLD: A.E. & L.A. Peters Outreach Enterprises, 2013.

Roberts, Oral. *Miracle of Seed-Faith.* New Jersey: Spire books, Fleming H. Revell, 1970.